THE
DICTIONARY
OF
BASEBALL

BY

Parke Cummings

Author of "The Dictionary of Sports"

o

WITH THE OFFICIAL RULES

o

A. S. BARNES and COMPANY

New York

INTRODUCTION

HEREIN are terms used in baseball, defined in their alphabetical order, together with the rules of the game, which underwent major revision in 1950. Since the rules section defines many terms, the advisability of listing them separately from the rules may be questioned. The answer is that only a small fraction of baseball terminology is what might be called "official." For example, the rules define a fair ball but do not define "triple," "scatter-arm," "free ticket," and many others used in daily baseball parlance.

In addition, certain of the structure of organized baseball is broken down in the text preceding the rules. All major league and AAA teams are listed, their nicknames given, and other leagues and classifications are itemized. None of this information, of course, may be found in the official rules of the game.

Preceding the text are listed the symbols and abbreviations used in the sport. The text itself is arranged in strictly alphabetical order, and operates as though all words in a compound term were run together, thus: **bat, bat around, bat boy, bat rack, batsmanship, batter.** In some cases both verb and noun meanings are given, as with **bat.** Cross-references are supplied with certain complex terms. Slang terms are followed with (s). Specifications are included, such as permissible size of equipment, distances between bases and the like. Typical box scores, league standings, averages and a scorecard are reproduced. At the start of the rules section there is a diagram of the field, and insets of home plate and the pitcher's mound.

This book is intended to explain the *structure* of the game, but not its history. Names of players, and their records, are accordingly not included, since to do so could expand its contents almost indefinitely. Its fundamental purpose is to explain what the game of baseball *is*—every phase of it—and to enable the reader to understand any term he may see in a publication or hear in conversation, or over broadcasts or telecasts—in short, to know the "lingo."

Parke Cummings

Westport, Conn.

SYMBOLS AND ABBREVIATIONS

Symbols

—	Base hit (on a scorecard).	3b.,	Third base.
=	Two base hit (on a score-card).	3B,	Three base hits.
≡	Three base hit (on a score-card).	4,	Second baseman (on a score-card).
≣	Home run (on a scorecard).	5,	Third baseman (on a score-card).
1,	Pitcher (on a scorecard).		
1b.,	First base.	6,	Shortstop (on a scorecard).
2,	Catcher (on a scorecard).	7,	Left fielder (on a scorecard).
2b.,	Second base.	8,	Center fielder (on a score-card).
2B,	Two base hits.		
3,	First baseman (on a score-card).	9,	Right fielder (on a score-card).

Abbreviations

a.,	Assists (sometimes capi-talized).	ER,	Earned runs.
		ERA,	Earned run average.
A,	Fumbled grounder (on a scorecard).	FC,	Fielder's choice.
ab.,	At bat (sometimes capi-talized).	G,	Games (played by a team or individual).
B,	Passed ball (on a score-card).	GIDP,	Grounded into double plays.
BB,	Bases on balls.	Gr. into DP	Same as the above.
BK,	Balks.	h.,	Base hits.
c.,	Catcher.	H,	Sacrifice hit (on a score-card).
cf.,	Center field.		
CG,	Completed games (by a given pitcher).	HB,	Hit batters (the num-ber a given pitcher has hit).
CS,	Caught stealing.		
DP,	Double plays.	HP,	Hit by pitcher (the number of times a given batter has been hit).
e.,	Errors (sometimes capi-talized).		
		HR,	Home runs.

v

if.,	Infielder.	r.,	Runs (sometimes capitalized).
IP,	Innings pitched (by a given pitcher).	RBI,	Runs batted in.
K,	Struck out (on a scorecard).	rf.,	Right field.
L,	Lost (number of games by a given team).	S,	Stolen base (on a scorecard).
LB,	Left on base.	SB,	Stolen bases.
lf.,	Left field.	SH,	Sacrifice hits.
O,	Muffed fly (on a scorecard).	SLG PC,	Slugging percentage.
of.,	Outfielder.	SO,	Strikeouts.
OR,	Opponents' runs.	ss.,	Shortstop.
p.,	Pitcher.	T,	Tied (number of games by a given team).
PB,	Passed balls (the number a given catcher is charged with).	TB,	Total bases.
		TC,	Total chances.
PC,	Percentage.	W,	1. Won. 2. Wild throw (on a scorecard).
po.,	Putouts (sometimes capitalized).	WP,	Wild pitches.
		XX,	Forceout (on a scorecard).

A

A. 1. A minor league classification. There are four A leagues, the Central, Eastern, South Atlantic and Western (all of which see). **2.** The abbreviation for assist.

AA. A minor league classification. There are two AA leagues, the Southern Association and the Texas League (both of which see).

AAA. The highest minor league classification, ranking next to the major leagues. There are three AAA leagues, the American Association, the International League, and the Pacific Coast League (all of which see).

aboard, (s)* adv. On base. Two men on base: "two aboard."

adjudged. Pertaining to a judgment decision by the umpire.

advance, v. To gain one or more bases.

afterpiece, (s) n. The second game of a double-header.

ahead, adv. Holding a lead or advantage, used notably for the relative ball and strike count. With 1 ball and 2 strikes, the pitcher is ahead of the batter. With 3 balls and 1 strike, the batter is ahead of the pitcher. Conversely the batter and pitcher are respectively "behind" in these instances.

all out, (s). The retirement of the side. "Three out, all out."

all-star, adj. Composed of star players. An all-star game between star players of the American and National League is annually played early in July.

* (s) slang.

American Association. An AAA minor league consisting of the Columbus Red Birds, the Indianapolis Indians, the Kansas City Blues, the Louisville Colonels, the Milwaukee Brewers, the Minneapolis Millers, the St. Paul Saints and the Toledo Mud Hens. The other two AAA leagues are the International League and the Pacific Coast League.

American Junior League. An organization for young ball players, organized by the American Legion. Over 1,000,000 players compete for a national junior championship.

American League. One of the two major leagues (the other is the National), consisting of the Boston Red Sox, Chicago White Sox, Cleveland Indians, Detroit Tigers, New York Yankees, Philadelphia Athletics, St. Louis Browns and Washington Senators.

Angels. The Los Angeles team of the Pacific Coast League (AAA). A "Southern" team.

appeal, n. The act of defensive player in claiming violation of the rules by the offensive team. In certain instances the umpire rules on these violations *only* if the defense appeals. Notable appeal plays: batting out of turn, failure to touch or retouch bases, overrunning or over-sliding first base and failing immediately to return thereto. See Rules 2.02, 6.06(e), 7.02, 7.08(d), and 7.10.

apple, (s). The ball.

arbiter, (s). An umpire.

around the horn, (s). A force double play in which the third baseman fields the ball and throws it to second base, after which it is relayed to first base.

A's, (s). A nickname for the Philadelphia Athletics.

ash, (s). A bat.

assist, n. A credit given in the scoring to a fielder who assists a teammate to make a putout or whose assistance would have resulted in a putout if the teammate had not erred. Example: A shortstop is credited with an assist for fielding a ground ball and throwing it to first base in time to retire the runner. Abbreviation: a. See Rule 10.08.

assist, v. To make a play which awards the player an assist.

at bat. Technically "a time at bat." The number of batting turns of a player during a game or season, charged to him with these exceptions: when hit by a pitched ball or receiving a base on balls; when he makes a sacrifice hit; when he is interfered with by the catcher. Abbreviation: ab. See Rules 6.04, 10.03 (a).

Athletics. The Philadelphia team of the American League (major). An "Eastern" team.

away. The number of men out in an inning. Two out: "two away."

B

B. A minor league classification next below A which nominally—though by no means invariably—applies to cities between 250,000 and 1,000,000 population. Included are the Big State, Carolina, Colonial, Florida International, Inter-State, Piedmont, Southeastern, Three-I, Tri-State and Western International Leagues.

backstop, n. 1. A screened structure behind the plate to stop foul balls from going into the stands. In big league baseball it must be at least 60′ behind home plate. Many teams also have smaller movable backstops to eliminate the need for a catcher in batting practice. 2. A term often applied to the catcher.

back up, v. To stand behind a teammate in position to retrieve a ball that might elude him. Example:

a pitcher goes behind home plate to back up the catcher on a throw from the outfield.

bad, (s) adj. A ball not pitched in the strike zone. A batter who habitually swings at such is a "bad ball hitter."

bag, n. First, second or third base. See BASE.

balk, n. 1. An infraction of the pitching rules with one or more runners on base. Most common balks: motion to throw to the plate or a base without doing so, while one foot is in contact with the pitcher's rubber; throwing to a base without first stepping directly toward it. Penalty: All runners advance one base. See Rules 2.04, 5.09(c), 7.04(a), 8.05. Abbreviation: BK. 2. Interference with the batter by the catcher or running out in front of the plate to catch a pitched ball. See Rule 6.07(c), 7.04(c & d), 7.07.

balk, v. To commit a balk.

BALL

ball, n. 1. A baseball. It has a cork or rubber center, wound with twine, and covered with bleached white horsehide or leather, stitched together. The major league ball must weigh not less than 5 nor more than 5¼ oz., and measure not less than 9″ nor more than 9¼″ in circumference. See Rule 1.03. 2. A pitch which does not enter the strike zone in flight and is not struck at by the batter. The term is put in quotes: "ball." See STRIKE ZONE and Rule 2.05.

ball hawk, (s). A fielder who gets a quick start toward a batted ball, notably an excellent outfielder.

balloon ascension, (s). A loss of effectiveness, as when a pitcher "blows up."

balloon ball, (s). A pitched ball, arching high into the air and descending as it crosses the plate —a type of slow delivery difficult for some batters to time correctly.

ball park. A baseball field, including the seating accommodations.

Baltimore chop, (s). A grounder that hits the ground relatively near the plate, then describes a long slow arc before descending, consuming so much time that the batter can often beat it out for an infield hit.

Baltimore Orioles. The Baltimore team of the International League (AAA). A "Southern" team.

banish, (s) v. To eject a player from the game (by the umpire).

barnstorm, (s) v. To make a playing tour after the regular season is ended, usually by a combination of players from various clubs.

base, n. One of the four objectives to be touched or occupied by runners on their legal advance to home base and a score. See FIRST BASE, SECOND BASE, THIRD BASE, HOME PLATE. The four bases are the corners of a 90′ square and all four are entirely within fair territory. First, second and third bases must be white canvas bags, 15″ square, not less than 3″ nor more than 5″ thick, filled with soft material and securely fastened in place at the points specified by the rules. Home plate is an imbedded five-sided rubber slab. See diagram at the beginning of the Rules. See Rules 1.10, 2.06.

baseball, n. 1. A team game, often called America's "national game," and popular in many other countries. It is played on a large field of which the most important part comprises the infield or "diamond"—four bases which are corners of a 90′ square. Teams of nine players compete in a game which normally consists of nine innings. During each half-inning one team occupies defensive positions in the field, and the other one takes turns at bat. The batter stands near home plate and is pitched to by the pitcher who stands approximately in the middle of the diamond. The batter's objective is to hit the ball into fair territory and away from a fielder and to reach first or any farther base before the ball can be thrown there, and eventually to complete the circuit and score a run by touching home plate. A player may be put out by striking out, by being tagged when off a base, by hitting a ball that is caught before it hits the ground, by being forced, and for other reasons. The batting side bats in rotation until three of its players are put out. It then takes fielding positions, and the opponents bat under the same conditions. The objective is to score the most runs in the game, each team being given an equal number of innings unless one less suffices at the end of the game for the team batting last.

The game is a major spectator sport when contested between professional teams representing large cities, and is played between smaller cities and towns, colleges, schools, clubs, etc., not to speak of informal "sandlot" games between boys. In the latter case, when smaller numbers of players are available, the game may be a variation. See ROUNDERS and cross-references under that term. A formal game requires officials (umpires) to call balls and strikes, rule on close plays at bases and make other decisions.

It is an impossibility to state *precisely* how the game originated. It may be stated however that: 1. baseball is not *solely* of American origin (as was basketball, for instance), but derives, at least in part, from cricket and rounders; 2. American modifications made it the game it is today;

3. in its basic recognizable modern essentials, the game may be dated back to the decade between 1840 and 1850.

All terms herein are, of course pertinent to baseball, but among the more essential ones are ASSIST, BALL, BASE, BASEBALL FIELD, BAT, BATTER, BATTING, BASE HIT, CATCH, CATCHER, ERROR, FAIR, FAIR BALL, FORCE, FOUL, FOUL BALL, FOUL LINE, GAME, GLOVE, HOME PLATE, INFIELD, INFIELDER, INNING, OUT, OUTFIELD, OUTFIELDER, PITCHER, PITCHER'S PLATE, PITCHING, PUTOUT, RUN, SAFE, STRIKE, STRIKEOUT, TAG, TEAM, UMPIRE. The diagram of the field, plus insets, is reproduced at the start of the Rules section. See Rule 1.01.

2. The ball used in baseball. See BALL, 1.

baseball field. A large level area, most of it as a rule, turfed, suitable in size and equipment for baseball. No precise size or shape is necessary, but major league rules call for a distance of at least 60' from home plate to any obstruction or stand in foul territory, 250' in fair territory. Distances in the latter often exceed 300', in some instances 400'. The field is divided into the infield and the outfield, the former standardized. It is a 90' square with bases at each corner, and is oriented from home plate, a five-sided rubber slab set in the ground. Two foul lines, at right angles, extend from its apex, and first and third base are located on them, each 90' from home plate. Second base, at the opposite corner from home plate, is 127′ 3⅜″ therefrom. The pitcher's plate, located on a mound 15″ high, is 60′ 6″ from home plate on a line with second base. Because of this orientation the square is called a "diamond," although it is not actually one. The territory between the bases on which players run (base paths) is unturfed, as well as that surrounding home plate. The outfield is the territory beyond the infield, roughly that beyond where the base paths extend. There are no fixtures therein. Territory outside the foul lines is foul territory. All four bases are entirely within fair territory. Lines demark where batters, coaches and catchers must stand. Some diamonds may be "skin" diamonds, being devoid of grass. In some cases, notably playgrounds, the entire field may be grassless. See the diagram at the start of the rules section; also HOME PLATE, FIRST BASE, SECOND BASE, THIRD BASE, PITCHER'S PLATE, FOUL LINE, BATTER'S BOX CATCHER'S BOX, COACHER'S BOX.

base hit. A fair hit which enables the batter to reach first base safely, provided he is not benefited by an error, and further provided that no base-runner is forced out on the play. Even if the attempted forceout fails, a base hit is awarded only if the scorer judges that the batter could not have been retired at first base by perfect fielding. An extra-base hit is scored as a base hit in compiling batting averages. Abbreviation: h. See Rules 10.04, 10.05.

base knock, (s). A base hit.

base line. The boundary within which the runner must keep when running between bases, being a space within three feet of a direct line between the bases, and thus 6′ wide. This boundary is not actually marked except for the three-foot line (which see). The runner may run outside the base line only when attempting to avoid a fielder who is fielding a batted ball. See Rule 7.08(a).

baseman, n. strictly one who plays first, second or third base. In effect the shortstop is also a baseman, since he often covers second base.

base on balls. The batter's privilege of going to first base if four "balls" are thrown to him before he is out for any cause or safely reaches base by other means. In that case he is not charged as being at bat. Abbreviation: bb. See Rule 2.07.

base path. The unturfed territory on part of which runners habitually run between bases. No rule defines it, but it usually includes more than the actual base line. See BASE LINE.

base-runner, n. An offensive player who is advancing toward, or touching, or returning to any base. Actually the batter becomes a base-runner before he reaches first base, becoming so instantly when he makes a fair hit, receives a base on balls or for any other cause that enables him to reach first base or legally attempt to do so. See Rules 2.59, 6.08.

base-running, n. The process of running from base to base, including such skills as leading, sliding, dodging or any others contributing to efficiency.

bases full. The situation when first, second and third base are each occupied by a runner. Also called bases "loaded," "jammed," "crammed," "packed," etc.

base umpire. An umpire at a base rather than behind home plate. Technically a field umpire. For duties see Rule 9.09.

bat, n. The implement with which the batter bats the ball. It must be round, not over 2¾″ in diameter at the thickest part, not more than 42″ long, and entirely of hardwood in one piece. Twine may be wound around it, or a granulated substance applied, for a maximum distance of 18″ from the handle. A majority of big league players use bats 34″-35″ long, and 36″ is rarely exceeded. The usual weight is 34-36 oz. The most common and satisfactory wood is ash. See Rule 1.14.

BAT

bat, v. To strike the ball with the bat or to fulfill any of the functions of the batter. See BATTER and BATTING.

bat around. To have all nine batters in the batting order come to bat in a given inning.

bat boy. A youth who tends the players' bats and other equipment.

bat rack. A rack in which bats are placed.

batsmanship, n. The skill or ability of a batter.

batter, n. The player who takes his place within the batter's box in his proper turn in the batting order. Function: To attempt to hit the ball delivered by the pitcher. Objectives: To get on base by a base hit, base on balls or any other means; to advance runners already on the bases and score them if possible. He may be put out if he strikes out, hits a ball that is caught on the fly, is forced or tagged. See BATTING, STRIKEOUT, BASE HIT, BASE ON BALLS, FORCE, STRIKE, BALL, FAIR BALL, FOUL BALL, BUNT. Rules 6.01-6.08 inclusive are pertinent to the batter.

batter's box. The lines within which the batter must stand when he takes his turn at bat. They form a rectangular box 6′ x 4′, there being a box on each side of home base, one for right-handed batters, the other for left-handed ones. Each box is 6″ from the nearest side of home plate, and the middle of the long side is on a line with the middle corners of the plate. See inset diagram at the beginning of the rules. Also see Rules 2.09, 6.06.

batter's circle. A circle, in foul territory in which the man "on deck" (the one following the actual batter) stands or squats. No rule specifies or defines it, but there are usually two such in big parks, each to accommodate players in the dugout nearest it.

Batter up! A command similar to "Play!"

battery, n. The pitcher and the catcher.

batting, n. The act of participating as batter. A right-handed batter's stance is with the left foot toward the pitcher's plate. The bat is gripped with both hands, often touching or close together, at or near the extremity of the handle, the left hand below the right one. Extensive, some or no preliminary "wagging" may be employed before the ball is pitched, depending on the batter's habits. Shortly before the pitch the bat is swung back and off the shoulders and is then swung forward, more or less on a line with the flight of the pitch, a forward stride taken with the left foot. Such are general rules; the batter's distance from the plate, the width of his stance, length of his stride or grip, trajectory and length of swing vary widely depending on his habits, objectives, the nature of the expected or actual pitch, etc. He may decide not to swing at the ball or may halt the swing before actually striking at it. See BATTER and accompanying cross-references.

batting average. The percentage efficiency of a batter, determined by the number of base hits he makes divided by his times at bat, carried out to three decimal places. Example: 100 hits in 300 times at bat: .333. Where the remaining fraction is one-half or over, a full point is added to the average. Example: Should a four-decimal figure show .3247, the batter's average is .325. See AT BAT and BASE HIT.

This batting standing, a final but unofficial one, shows how av-

Major League Leaders

FINAL STANDINGS
Batters
AMERICAN LEAGUE

	G.	AB.	R.	H.	PC
Kell, Detroit	134	522	99	179	.3429
Williams, Boston	155	566	150	194	.34275
Dillinger, St. Louis	137	545	69	176	.323
Mitchell, Cleveland	149	641	81	203	.317
Doerr, Boston	140	546	92	169	.310
Michaels, Chicago	154	561	73	173	.310
DiMaggio, Boston	145	605	126	186	.307
Pesky, Boston	148	603	111	185	.307
Sievers, St. Louis	140	471	84	144	.306
Wertz, Detroit	155	608	96	185	.304

NATIONAL LEAGUE

	G.	AB.	R.	H.	PC
Robinson, Brooklyn	156	593	122	203	.342
Musial, St. Louis	157	611	129	207	.339
Slaughter, St. Louis	151	568	92	191	.336
Furillo, Brooklyn	142	549	95	177	.322
Kiner, Pittsburgh	151	549	115	170	.310
Thomson, New York	156	641	99	198	.309
Kluszewski, Cincinnati	135	529	69	163	.308
Marshall, New York	141	499	82	153	.307
Ennis, Philadelphia	154	611	92	184	.301
H. Walker, Chic-Cincin	127	472	72	142	.301

—*Courtesy of the New York Times.*

erages are determined. Being a final one, it is an exception to the rule about adding a full point for a fourth-decimal fraction of one-half or over. That rule would place both Williams' and Kell's average at .343, but to determine the champion for the year, the figures are carried out until a tie is broken. The G. and the R. columns represent games played in and runs scored, but are not relevant to the actual batting average. This is determined solely by dividing the AB (at bat) figures in the H. (base hit) ones.

batting order. The order, designated by the manager, coach or captain (manager in big league play) in which members of a team shall take their turns at bat. It cannot be changed during a game; a substitute batter, or his subsequent substitute, must retain the place in the batting order of the player he displaced. Violation often results in a player being declared out. See rules 4.01 (a & c), 4.04, 6.01, 6.06(e).

batting out of turn. See BATTING ORDER.

batting practice. Practice in batting, usually held before a game. The pitcher is often a "batting practice pitcher," who seldom starts regular games, and a small, movable backstop is often substituted for the catcher.

batting team. The team at bat.

bean ball, (s). A ball pitched at or near the batter's head in an effort to frighten him away from the plate. When intentional it is illegal. See DUSTER, and Rule 8.02 (c).

beat out. To make a hit by beating a fielder's throw to first base.

Beavers. The Portland (Oregon) team of the Pacific Coast League (AAA). A "Northern" team.

beef, (s) n. A heated protest at a decision.

beef, (s) v. To make a beef.

behind, adv. Lagging or at a disadvantage, used notably for the relative ball and strike count. With 1 ball and 2 strikes, the batter is behind the pitcher. With 3 balls and 1 strike, the pitcher is behind the batter. Conversely the pitcher and batter are respectively ahead in these instances.

bench, n. A bench on which substitutes as well as playing members of the batting team sit. In major league play the bench is located in the dugout.

bench, (s) v. To remove from the line-up or to demote a former regular starting player to substitute status.

bench jockey, (s). A player who "jockeys" (taunts) the opponents from the bench, notably one with marked talent for such jockeying.

bender, (s) n. A curve ball. A term not often used in modern times.

Bengals, (s). A nickname for the Detroit Tigers.

big league. A term which may be applied in general to any league of substantial importance, but usually specifically applied to the two major leagues (American and National).

bingle, (s) n. A base hit.

Bisons. The Buffalo (N.Y.) team of the International League (AAA). A "Northern" team.

blank, (s) v. To shut out, i.e., prevent the opponents from scoring.

bleacherite, (s) n. One who sits in the bleachers.

bleachers, n. Uncovered stands, usually surrounding certain outfield sections, hence more cheaply priced and usually unreserved.

bleeder, (s) n. A scratch hit, notably one not hit solidly or hit on the handle of the bat.

blooper, (s) n. 1. A batted ball, not solidly hit, which travels in an arc. It may land beyond the infielders and in front of the outfielders for a hit. 2. See BALLOON BALL.

blow, (s) v. To lose a contest, make a bad misplay or a bad decision (by umpire).

blow up, (s). To lose effectiveness, notably by a pitcher.

blue-darter, (s) n. A sharply hit ball, through or over the infield. Not a long drive.

Bluejays, (s). A nickname applied to the Philadelphia Phillies.

Blues. The Kansas City (Mo.) team of the American Association (AAA). A "Western" team.

bobble, (s) n. An error in catching or handling the ball, or momentarily juggling it.

bobble, (s) v. To make a bobble.

Bombers, (s). A nickname for the New York Yankees.

bone, (s) n. A foolish play. An error in judgment. Also called "bone-head play," or "boner."

boot, (s) v. To make an error in fielding a ground ball, notably if the ball is accidentally kicked.

Bosox, (s). A nickname for the Boston Red Sox.

Boston Braves. A major league team, being an "Eastern" one in the National League. Home grounds: Braves Field.

Boston Red Sox. A major league team, being an "Eastern" one in the American League. Home grounds: Fenway Park.

bottom, n. The second, or home, half of an inning.

box, n. A term applied to various confines in which players or squad members stand, such as the pitcher's box, batter's box, catcher's box, coacher's box. See Pitcher's Plate, Pitcher's Mound, Catcher's Box, Coacher's Box, Batter's Box.

boxman, (s) n. A pitcher.

box score. A condensed summary of the game, like the one herewith reproduced.

The Box Score

BROOKLYN (N.)	ab.	r.	h.	po.	a.	e.
Reese, ss.....	5	1	1	0	1	0
Jorg'sen, 3b...	3	1	1	2	2	0
aEdwards....	1	0	0	0	0	0
Miksis, 3b...	0	0	0	1	2	0
Snider, cf....	4	1	1	2	0	0
Robi'son, 2b..	3	1	1	1	2	0
H'm'nski, lf...	3	1	0	0	0	0
Olmo, lf....	2	0	1	2	0	0
Furillo, rf....	6	2	4	4	0	1
Hodges, 1b...	4	2	2	10	1	0
Camp'ella, c..	3	0	1	7	0	0
N'combe, p...	2	0	1	1	0	0
Barney, p.....	1	0	0	0	0	0
Banta, p......	1	0	0	0	1	0
Total......	38	9	13	30	9	1

PHILADELPHIA (N.)	ab.	r.	h.	po.	a.	e.
Ashburn, cf..	6	0	2	4	0	0
eSanicki.....	1	0	0	0	0	0
Hamner, ss..	5	1	1	4	5	0
Sisler, 1b....	4	0	1	11	2	1
Ennis, lf.....	4	2	2	0	0	0
Seminick, c..	5	0	0	1	1	1
Nich'son, rf..	4	1	1	2	0	0
Jones, 3b....	5	1	1	1	4	0
Goliat, 2b...	5	1	2	6	0	0
Meyer, p....	0	0	0	1	0	0
Roberts, p...	0	0	0	0	0	0
bBlatner....	0	0	0	0	0	0
Th'mpson, p.	0	0	0	0	0	0
cHollmig....	1	0	1	0	0	0
Simmons, p..	0	0	0	0	0	0
K'nstanty, p.	0	0	0	0	0	0
dBlatnik....	1	1	1	0	0	0
H'zelman, p.	1	0	0	0	2	0
Trinkle, p...	0	0	0	0	0	0
Total.....	42	7	12	30	14	2

a Flied out for Jorgensen in seventh.
bWalked for Roberts in third.
cDoubled for Thompson in fourth.
dSingled for Konstanty in sixth.
eStruck out for Trinkle in tenth.

Brooklyn.....................0 0 5 0 2 0 0 0 0 2—9
Philadelphia.................0 0 0 4 1 2 0 0 0 0—7

Runs batted in—Robinson, Furillo, Hodges, Campanella 2, Snider, Olmo, Jones 3, Ashburn, Nicholson, Hamner, Ennis.
Two-base hits—Hollmig, Campanella, Nicholson, Home run—Jones. Sacrifices—Banta, Robinson, Miksis. Stolen bases—Robinson 2. Double play—Hamner and Sisler. Left on bases—Brooklyn 12, Philadelphia 9. Bases on balls—Off Meyer 3, Roberts 1, Newcombe 2, Thompson 1, Barney 1, Konstanty 1, Heintzelman 4, Banta 1. Struck out—By Newcombe 2, Barney 1, Konstanty 1, Banta 3. Hits—Off Meyer 5 in 2 2-3 innings, Roberts 1 in 1-3, Thompson 0 in 1, Simmons 2 in 0, Newcombe 6 in 3 1-3, Barney 4 in 2 1-3, Banta 2 in 4 1-3, Konstanty 1 in 2, Heintzelman 4 in 3 1-3, Trinkle 0 in 2-3. Wild pitch—Meyer 2. Winner—Banta (10—6). Loser—Heintzelman (17—10). Umpires—Goetz, Reardon, Barlick and Jorda. Time of game—3:17. Attendance—36,765.

—*Courtesy of the New York Times.*

Printing of the Philadelphia section on the right indicates that it was the home team, as also does printing Philadelphia below Brooklyn in the inning summary. The notation (N.) after the names indicate they are National League teams. Accomplishments are listed after the name of players as are their positions. Reese, first in the batting order for Brooklyn, played shortstop. He was officially at bat 5 times, scored 1 run, made 1 base hit, no putouts, 1 assist, no errors. The lines marked total give the aggregate team accomplishments, and the figures under the r. (run) column reveal that Brooklyn won 9-7. The inning summary likewise indicates this, and further reveals that the game went 10 innings, since there are 10 sets of figures. The score was 7-7 at the end of the ninth inning. Brooklyn won by making 2 runs in the first half of the tenth, while Philadelphia failed to score. Actual substitutes who take fielder's positions are listed in the first section of the box score. For instance Olmo substituted for Hermanski ("H'm'nski" due to space restrictions) as a left fielder. Pinch hitters (and pinch runners, should there have been any) are identified in different fashion. The a in front of Edwards' name is a reference to a subsequent item which reveals he batted for Jorgensen in the seventh and was put out on a caught fly ball (a Flied out for Jorgensen in seventh). No position abbreviation follows Edwards' name, so we know he did not subsequently take the field. After the inning summary are other pertinent details of the game. There were many pitchers on each team, and the official scorer decreed that Banta was the winning pitcher, Heintzelman the losing one. See WINNING PITCHER and LOSING PITCHER. Figures in parentheses after their names indicate their seasonal record. Banta won 10 games and lost 6 during the season, this game included.

Braves. The Boston team of the National League (major). An "Eastern" team.

Braves Field. Home grounds of the Boston Braves. Distance from home plate to right field: 320'; center field: 390'; left field: 337'.

breadbasket catch, (s). A catch similar to a "vest pocket catch" (which see).

break, v. A term with several meanings in baseball. 1. A pitched ball breaks when it curves or changes direction. 2. A runner breaks when he starts suddenly toward a base. 3. A batter is said to "break" his wrists when he takes an intentional swing at the ball, rather than halting it half-way through.

break, (s) n. A lucky or unlucky occurrence (depending on the viewpoint), such as a grounder hitting a pebble and bouncing over an infielder's head.

breeze, (s) v. 1. To win easily. 2. To pitch a fast ball. The pitcher "breezes" one past the batter.

Brewers. The Milwaukee team of the American Association (AAA). A "Western" team.

Briggs Stadium. Home grounds of the Detroit Tigers. Distance from home plate to right field: 325'; center field: 420'; left field: 340'.

Bronx Bombers, (s). A nickname for the New York Yankees.

Bronx cheer, (s). A derisive sound made by compression of the lips. So named for its popularity with the citizenry of that New York City borough, many of them loyal baseball fans.

Brooklyn Dodgers. A major league team, being an "Eastern" one in the National League. Home grounds: Ebbets Field.

Brownies, (s). A nickname for the St. Louis Browns.

Browns. The St. Louis team of the American League (major). A "Western" team.

Buffalo Bisons. An International League (AAA) team. A "Northern" team.

bullpen, (s) n. A piece of ground, often fenced off in an outfield region, where relief pitchers or substitutes may warm up without interfering with the progress of the game.

Bums, (s). A nickname for the Brooklyn Dodgers.

bunt, n. A legally batted ball, not swung at, but intentionally met with the bat and tapped slowly within the infield, usually to advance a runner, sometimes to reach first base as a surprise maneuver. The bat is usually choked, the hands somewhat farther apart. A foul bunt on the third strike puts the batter out. See SACRIFICE HIT, SQUEEZE PLAY and Rules 2.12, 6.05(c).

bunt, v. To make a bunt.

bunting, n. 1. That done when one bunts. 2. The pennant.

busher, (s) n. A bush league player. See BUSH LEAGUE.

bush league, (s). A small minor league.

butterfly, (s) n. See BALLOON BALL.

C

C. A minor league classification next below B which nominally— though by no means invariably— applies to cities between 150,000 and 250,000 population. Included are the Arizona-Texas, Border, California, and Canadian-American Leagues, the Central Association, the Cotton States, East Texas, Evangeline, Gulf Coast, Middle Atlantic, Northern, Pioneer, Rio Grande Valley, Sunset Leagues, the Western Association and the West Texas-New Mexico League.

cage, n. 1. A movable backstop. 2. A large building where baseball may be practiced indoors. Used by certain colleges.

called game. A game in which because of darkness, rain or other legal reason, an umpire-in-chief terminates play.

can of corn, (s). A high fly ball which, however, merely ends up by being caught for an out.

canto, (s) n. An inning.

cap, n. The vizored head covering worn in baseball, usually decorated with the team's initials or insignia.

captain, n. A term usually applied in baseball to a player who has certain duties of leadership but is usually secondary to the manager (professional) or coach (amateur). In the official rules the term "manager or captain" is sometimes used. See MANAGER and accompanying cross-references.

Cardinals. The St. Louis team of the National League (major). A "Western" team.

Cards, (s). A nickname for the St. Louis Cardinals.

catch, v. 1. To secure and hold a ball. In baseball the term often applies to a ball caught on the fly as opposed to a batted one caught on the bounce. 2. To play the position of catcher.

catch, n. A caught ball, so caught only in the hand or glove, and held long enough to prove that the player has complete control of it. See Rule 2.14.

catcher, n. The player who stands behind home base, and who catches, or attempts to catch, pitched balls not hit by the batter. Other duties are to signal the type of pitch; to throw to bases, notably to prevent stolen bases; to tag out, if possible, any runner who attempts to score; to back up other fielders if necessary. The position was formerly unrestricted by rule, although in modern baseball the catcher has always stood close behind the plate. Now the modern rule compels him to stand within the catcher's box. See CATCHER'S BOX. The mitt is unrestricted as to size and shape, and a large round heavily-padded one is worn. Rules do not make a mask, body protector and shinguards compulsory, but these are invariably worn in adult play of any appreciable caliber. The position is of great importance, and the catcher virtually "runs" the team since he usually decrees the type of pitch which in turn often determines the defensive alignments and the tactics. The catcher is usually of sturdy build, adept at catching or blocking all types of pitches and in guarding the plate against runners. He should have a strong arm capable of making line throws to bases, and good tactical judgment, including ability to anticipate opponents' moves, and a knowledge of the opposing batters' likes and dislikes. Abbreviation: c. See Rules 2.15, 2.16.

catcher's balk. Catcher's interference (which see) when a base-runner attempts to score from third base.

catcher's box. A right-angled isosceles triangle behind home plate in which the catcher must stand when a pitch is delivered. Its top apex, the right angle, is formed by the intersection of the foul lines at the plate, both of them continued in back of the plate. At a point 8' behind home plate, on an imaginary line with second base, a line is drawn at right angles to this imaginary line, continuing 8' in each direction where it intersects the continuations of the foul lines. The triangle therefore has a 16' base, and its other two sides are each about 11' 4" long. See inset at beginning of rules section and Rule 2.16.

catcher's interference. Interference with the batter by the catcher, such as tipping his bat or pushing him. The batter is awarded first base, the catcher is charged with an error, and the batter is not charged with a time at bat. Should a base-runner be attempting to steal a base, he is awarded that base. If an opponent is trying to steal home or to score on a squeeze play, both a balk and interference is called for pushing the batter, tipping his bat or running out in front of the plate to catch a pitched ball. The runner scores, and the batter is awarded first base. See Rules 2.04, 7.04, 7.07.

cellar, (s) n. Last place in a league or conference standing.

center field. 1. The outfield territory beyond second base and between that habitually covered by the right and left fielders. 2. The position designation of the player who covers such territory. Abbreviation: cf.

center fielder. The outfielder who covers center field territory, and plays the position of center field.

Central League. One of the four minor leagues in the A classification, the other three being the Eastern, South Atlantic and Western Leagues. There are six teams: Charleston, W. Va.; Dayton, Ohio; Flint, Mich.; Grand Rapids, Mich.; Muskegon, Mich.; Saginaw, Mich.

chain baseball. A system where a club gets first option on the service of certain teams in lower leagues. Major league teams often have such "farm" clubs in minor leagues.

chalk up, (s). To win. The pitcher chalks up a victory.

chance, n. A reasonable opportunity, as specified in the scoring rules, to field the ball. See TOTAL CHANCES.

change of pace. The ability to pitch balls of varying speed with the same motion, thereby often confusing the batter.

change-up, n. A change of pace.

chase, (s) v. 1. To cause a pitcher to be taken out because of heavy batting. 2. To eject a player from the game (by the umpire).

chest protector. An inflated pad usually worn over the front part of the body as protection from injury, used by the catcher and the plate umpire—especially to guard against foul tips.

Chicago Cubs. A major league team, being a "Western" one in the National League. Home grounds: Wrigley Field.

Chicago White Sox. A major league team, being a "Western" one in the American League. Home grounds: Comiskey Park.

Chiefs. The Syracuse team of the International League (AAA). A "Southern" team.

choke, v. To hold the bat shorter, i.e., farther from the handle.

choke up, (s). To lose efficiency because of emotional tenseness. The accusation has been leveled at both players and umpires.

chop, v. To swing at the ball with a somewhat downward stroke, resulting in a grounder. See also BALTIMORE CHOP.

Cincinnati Reds. A major league team, being a "Western" one in the National League. Home grounds: Crosley Field.

circle, n. See BATTER'S CIRCLE.

circle, v. To run around. A player scoring a run circles the bases.

circuit, n. 1. A league or conference. 2. The four bases. A player scoring a run completes the circuit.

circuit clout, (s). A home run.

class, n. The classification in which teams and leagues are placed because of skill or the size of the city. There are many classes in professional baseball. See MAJOR LEAGUE, AAA, AA, A, B, C, D.

clean, (s) v. To make a home run with men on base, the bases thus being "cleaned" of runners.

clean-up, (s) adj. The fourth position in the batting order, usually accorded a team's most powerful batter. So placed on the theory that he will be able to score teammates who get on base ahead of him.

clear, (s) v. The same as to "clean," (which see).

clearing the bench, (s). The removal, by the umpire, of all players on the bench for objectionable conduct when individual offenders cannot be detected. They must leave the bench and go to the clubhouse, but a manager or captain may send there for such substitutes as are actually needed to replace players in the game. See Rule 4.08.

Cleveland Indians. A major league team, being a "Western" one in the American League. Home grounds: Cleveland Municipal Stadium.

Cleveland Municipal Stadium. Home grounds of the Cleveland Indians. Distance from home plate to right field: 320′; center field: 412′; left field: 320′.

clinch, v. To be assured of the championship or any specific place in a league, regardless of subsequent events. Example: a team with a six-game lead and only five games remaining to play has clinched the championship since it could lose all remaining games and still finish ahead.

closed stance. A batting stance in which the right foot is pulled

back from an imaginary line between the pitcher's plate and home plate (for a right-handed batter). Left foot for a left-handed batter.

clout, (s) n. A hard-hit ball.

clout, (s) v. To bat hard. The batter "clouts" one.

clouter, (s) n. A heavy hitter.

club, n. 1. An organization, such as a professional ball club. 2. Slang for the bat.

clubhouse, n. The building in which players dress for the game, containing lockers, showers, etc.

clutch, (s) n. A desperate situation. The "pinch." A batter capable of delivering much-needed hits is a "clutch hitter."

coach, n. A term applied in baseball to an individual who coaches players in skills (as one who coaches them in practice) and also to the individual who occupies the coacher's box or lines. Technically he is the coacher (which see).

coach, v. To serve in the capacity of coach or coacher.

coacher, n. A member of the team at bat privileged to stand within the coacher's box and give instruction to base-runners and batters of his team. He need not be a player taking part in the game or even one on its roster of active players. There may be a coacher in each coacher's box. See Rules 2.17, 4.05, 5.08, 5.09(h), 7.09 (e & f).

coacher's box. Lines starting outside the diamond at first and third base, extending 20′ toward home plate, parallel to and 15′ from the base lines. At their extremities other lines are drawn perpendicular to them, extending 10′ toward the stands. They accordingly form a box in which the coacher must stand. See COACHER and accompanying cross-references. See also the diagram at the beginning of the playing rules.

Colonels. The Louisville team of the American Association (AAA). An "Eastern" team.

Columbus Red Birds. The Columbus team of the American Association (AAA). An "Eastern" team.

Comiskey Park. Home grounds of the Chicago White Sox. Distance from home plate to right field: 332′; center field: 420′; left field: 332′.

Corsairs, (s). A nickname for the Pittsburgh Pirates.

connect, (s) v. To hit the ball. The term usually implies it is met solidly for a hit. Context sometimes denotes a home run is meant.

count, n. The number of balls and strikes on the batter, usually recorded in that order. With 1 ball and 2 strikes, the count is "1 and 2." 3 balls and 2 strikes: "3 and 2," the latter also known as "full count."

counter, (s) n. A run.

cousin, (s) n. A term usually applied in baseball to a pitcher a certain team can consistently defeat, or to a pitcher a batter usually hits well.

cover, v. To play an assigned position, guarding a base or territory. A player "covers" a base.

cripple, (s) n. A pitch which the pitcher must get over the plate because he is behind in the count, such as 3 balls, 1 or no strikes.

Crosley Field. Home grounds of the Cincinnati Reds. Distance from home plate to right field: 342′; center field: 387′; left field: 328′.

crossfire, n. A delivery in which the pitcher, using a sidearm motion, releases the ball as far as possible to his side, thus causing it to travel toward the plate somewhat diagonally.

crowd, n. The number of spectators.

crowd, v. To stand close to the plate when batting.

Cubs. The Chicago team of the National League (major). A "Western" team. Also the Springfield team of the International League (AAA). A "Southern" team.

curtain-raiser, (s) n. The first game of a season or series; also the first game of a double-header.

curve, n. A pitched ball which changes direction instead of going straight, caused by spin imparted on the ball. See OUTCURVE, INCURVE.

curve, v. To throw a curve.

cushion, (s) n. 1. A comfortable lead. The pitcher goes into the ninth with a nine-run "cushion." 2. A base.

cut, v. 1. To pitch a ball over a corner of the plate, thus "cutting" a corner. 2. To fail to touch a base when running the bases. 3. To swing at a pitched ball. Take your "cut."

cut-off, n. An interception of a thrown ball by a teammate for whom the throw was not apparrently intended. Example: With a runner on second base certain to score on a base hit, an infielder cuts off the outfielder's throw to the plate in order to prevent the hitter reaching second base while a fruitless play is made at the plate.

cycle, (s) n. A player hits for the cycle when he makes a single, double, triple and home run (in any order) in a given game.

D

D. The lowest minor league classification which nominally—though by no means invariably—applies to cities of less than 150,000 population. Included are the Alabama State, Appalachian, Blue Ridge, Coastal Plain, Far West, Florida State, Georgia-Alabama, Georgia-Florida, Georgia State, Kansas-Oklahoma-Missouri (K-O-M), Kitty, Longhorn, Mississippi-Ohio Valley, Mountain States, North Atlantic, North Carolina State, Ohio-Indiana, Pennsylvania-Ontario-New York (Pony), Sooner State, Tobacco State, Virginia, Western Carolina and Wisconsin State Leagues.

daisy-cutter, (s) n. A hard-hit grounder.

dead ball. The situation when the ball is not in play. Among causes: batter hit by pitched ball; balk; an uncaught foul hit; interference; ball handled by spectator; a bat hitting a bunt or fair hit on fair ground; a fair hit touching a runner or umpire before it touches a fielder. See Rules 2.18, 3.14, 5.07, 5.09, 5.10.

deep, adv. Far out from the plate. Both outfielders and infielders may play deep.

deface, v. To mar the surface of the ball, punishable by removal from the game and a ten-day fine in the major leagues. See Rule 8.02(a).

defense, n. The team in the field. Likewise the quality of its fielding.

deliver, v. 1. To pitch. 2. (s) To come through in the "clutch."

delivery, n. The act of pitching. Likewise the caliber and type of the pitch.

derrick, (s) v. To remove a pitcher.

Detroit Tigers. A major league team, being a "Western" one in the American League. Home grounds: Briggs Stadium.

diamond, n. The quadrilateral (actually a square) formed by home, first, second and third bases. See BASEBALL FIELD and diagram at beginning of the rules.

die, (s) v. 1. To be left on base. 2 But less common, to be put out.

dish, (s) n. Home plate.

division, n. 1. A classification determined by standing in a league. In an eight-team league the four leading teams comprise the first division, the other four the second division. 2. A geographical classification for convenience in scheduling purposes. See EASTERN TEAM, WESTERN TEAM, NORTHERN TEAM, SOUTHERN TEAM.

Dixie Series. A four-out-of-seven series between the winners of the play-off series in the Southern Association and Texas League, therefore for the AA championship.

Dodgers. The Brooklyn team of the National League (major). An "Eastern" team.

double, n. A two base hit.

double, v. 1. To make a two base hit. 2. To make a double play. Also called to "double up."

double bill, (s). A double-header (which see).

doubled up. Retired by a double play, usually applied to the player retired last.

double-header, n. Two games played consecutively for one admission price, sometimes necessitated by previous postponements, sometimes scheduled in advance. Twenty minutes usually intervene between games. See Rules 2.20, 3.12(c), 4.12.

double play. A play by the defense in which two offensive players are legally put out as a result of continuous play. A common type of double play occurs, when, with a runner on first base, the batter hits a ground ball to a fielder who touches second base (or relays it to a teammate who does so), ahead of the runner who was on first. The play is then completed by throwing the ball to first base before the batter (now a base-runner) reaches it. The first runner was forced (see FORCE) at second base, the batter forced at first. But if the batter is retired first, the runner who was on first must be tagged out at second, since he was not forced. Another common type of double play: Runner on base: batter lines a fly ball to a fielder who relays it to the base before the runner can return there (as he must by the rule for a caught fly ball). A batted ball is *not* essential for a double play; the retirement of a would-be stealer on the same play in which the batter strikes out is a double play. Abbreviation: DP. See Rules 2.21, 10.09.

double steal. The accomplishment of two base-runners stealing bases on the same play. Example: Runners on first and third bases. The runner on first steals second, and the second baseman cannot relay the ball to the catcher in time to prevent the runner who was on third from scoring. See Rule 10.11(a).

double up. To complete a double play, the term usually applied to the second runner retired. A is put out and B is doubled up on the play.

down, adj. 1. Out. Two out: "two down." 2. Behind in the game score.

downer, (s) n. See DROP.

draft, n. A system by which a certain team gets first opportunity to sign up new players from lower leagues.

drag bunt. A soft bunt, made by pulling the bat back as the ball is hit, intended to "drag" slowly along the ground, and usually to beat out for a base hit.

draw, v. To make a fielder throw to a base. A runner, by taking a lead, may "draw" the throw, sometimes enabling a teammate to profit by it—or causing a wild throw.

drawn game. See TIE and REGULATION GAME.

drive, n. A hard hit ball.

drive, v. To bat the ball hard.

drop, (s) n. An overhand pitch which drops down as it nears the plate. Most, delivered by a right-handed pitcher to a right-handed batter, curve away from the batter as well as dropping. In mod-

ern times more often called "sinker" or "downer."

dugout, n. An enclosure for the player's bench. In big league baseball it must be roofed, and closed at the back and ends. It is usually of concrete. See Rules 1.12, 2.11, 2.22, 3.17, 4.08.

dust, (s) v. A term usually applied to pitching a ball close to a batter's head in an effort to scare him away from the plate. One interpretation differentiates this from the "bean ball" where the ball is deliberately thrown directly at the head, rather than close to it. See Rule 8.02(c).

duster, (s) n. A ball thrown with intention to "dust." See DUST.

dust off, (s). See DUST.

E

earned run. A run scored against a pitcher, provided it is not caused by a teammate's error. A relief pitcher is not charged for earned runs scored by base-runners who got on base against the preceding pitcher, nor one scored by the first batter he faces if that batter had any advantage due to poor pitching by the preceding pitcher —such as 2 or 3 balls and 1 or 0 strikes, or 3 balls and 2 strikes. It cannot be scored because of a batter reaching first by catcher's interference or a passed ball, nor can any run be earned after the fielding team has failed to accept chances that would have retired the team at bat. Thus if an error is made with 2 out, no succeeding runs are earned, even if made on legitimate hits. Abbreviation: ER. See Rule 10.15.

earned run average. The average of earned runs scored off a pitcher in a 9-inning game, determined by dividing the total number of earned runs off his pitching by the total number of innings he has pitched, and multiplying by 9. Example: pitcher has 233 innings pitched and gives up 58 earned runs. Former figure goes into the latter .2484 when carried to four places. Multiplying this by 9 gives 2.2356. Only two places beyond the decimal are used, so the latter two figures (56) make the earned run average 2.24. Abbreviation: ERA. See Rules 10.15, 10.17.

Eastern League. One of the four minor leagues in the A classification, the other three being the Central, South Atlantic and the Western. There are eight teams:

Albany, N. Y.; Binghamton, N. Y.; Elmira, N. Y.; Hartford, Conn.; Scranton, Pa.; Utica, N. Y.; Wilkes-Barre, Pa.; Williamsport, Pa.

Eastern team. A team classified as "Eastern" for scheduling purposes. In the American League the four Eastern teams are the Boston Red Sox, New York Yankees, Philadelphia Athletics and Washington Senators. National League: Boston Braves, Brooklyn Dodgers, New York Giants and Philadelphia Phillies. American Association: Columbus Red Birds, Indianapolis Indians, Louisville Colonels and Toledo Mud Hens.

Ebbets Field. Home grounds of the Brooklyn Dodgers. Distance from home plate to right field: 297′; center field: 393′; left field: 343′.

emery ball. A ball illegally roughed up or defaced. Its use, by the pitcher, is penalized by removal from the game and a ten-day suspension in major leagues. See Rule 8:02(a).

ephus, (s) n. See BALLOON BALL.

erase, (s) v. To put out.

F

fadeaway, n. A pitched ball that slows up and drops. The term is usually applied only to the delivery of pitcher, Christy Mathewson, credited with its invention.

fair, adj. Pertaining to the sector of the field between the two foul lines, including all parts of all four bases, the foul lines, the foul poles. See diagram at the beginning of the rules, and Rule 2.24.

error, n. A misplay by a fielder which prolongs the time at bat of the batter or prolongs the life of the base-runner or allows the latter to make one or more bases than a perfect play would have entitled him to. Among exceptions: a passed ball and a wild pitch. Inefficient pitching, such as a base on balls, hit batter, or balk, is likewise not in the error category. An error is not charged if, in the opinion of the scorer, a batted or thrown ball could not have been handled by the fielder even though he touched it. A ball can be "too hot to handle," or it may be batted so slowly toward an infielder that he would have insufficient time to retire the runner even with perfect handling. Abbreviation: E. See Rule 10.10.

exhibition, n. A game between teams which is not on a league schedule or is not a play-off or World Series game.

extra base hit. A two base hit, three base hit, or home run.

extra inning. Any inning after the ninth, or any inning after the prescribed number of innings contestants have agreed to play.

fair ball. A legally batted ball that settles on fair ground between home and first base; or between home and third base; or that is on or over fair ground when bounding to the outfield past first or third base, or that touches first or third base; or that first falls on fair ground on or beyond first or third base; or that, while on or over fair ground, touches an umpire or player. When a batted ball passes outside the playing field, the umpire rules it fair or foul according to where it leaves the playing field. See Rule 2.23.

fair ground. Any ground where the ball is fair (which see). Also called fair territory.

fair territory. See FAIR and FAIR GROUND.

fall-away slide. See HOOK SLIDE.

fan, n. An enthusiastic follower of the sport.

fan, (s) v. 1. To strike out, usually denoting that the third strike is swung on. Sometimes used to denote any strike swung on and missed. 2. To discuss baseball.

fanning bee, (s). A spirited baseball discussion.

far corner (s). Third base.

farm, (s) n. A club where players are developed, such as a minor league team where a certain major league team has first option on its players' services. A club with option on many such uses the "farm system," and when it sends players to lesser teams it "farms them out."

fast ball. An overhand pitch at top speed. The ball usually has a backward spin which causes it to rise or "hop" slightly.

fat, (s) adj. Large or readily seen. The "fat" part of the bat (the "good wood") is that part where the ball can be most effectively hit. A "fat" pitch is a relatively slow one with nothing on it— therefore easier to hit.

fence, n. Any fence surrounding the field. Major league rules decree that all such must be at least 250′ from home plate in fair territory, at least 60′ in foul.

fence-buster, (s) n. A heavy hitter.

Fenway Park. Home grounds of the Boston Red Sox. Distance from home plate to right field: 302′; center field: 420′; left field: 315′.

field, n. 1. See BASEBALL FIELD. 2. The defensive team, not at bat. It "takes the field."

field, v. To catch or secure a ball.

fielder, n. One in fielding position, the term not usually applied to the battery. See INFIELDER, OUTFIELDER.

fielder's choice. A situation when, with a man or men on base, a fielder, after handling a batted ball, elects to retire a base-runner instead of the batter. See Rule 10.04(i).

fielding average. A fielder's efficiency determined by dividing a fielder's total chances (putouts, assists, and errors) into his total of putouts and assists, and carrying out the result to three decimal points. Example: A fielder, in a season, makes 186 putouts, 345 assists and 20 errors for 551 total chances. 551 divided into 531 (total of putouts and assists), gives him a fielding average of .964. See Rule 10.17(d).

field umpire. An umpire, secondary to the umpire-in-chief, who takes a position best, in his judgment, to render decisions at the bases. Duties: To rule on base decisions; to rule on foreign substance on the ball and to prohibit freak deliveries; to aid the umpire-in-chief to enforce the rules, including the right to remove or fine a player. He has equal authority with the umpire-in-chief in calling balks. See Rule 9.09.

fine, n. A financial penalty imposed for misconduct. See Rules 3.08, 3.09, 3.11, 3.17, 4.13, 8.02 (c), 9.13.

fine, v. To impose a fine.

fingernail ball. A pitched ball gripped by the fingernails, acting somewhat like the knuckle ball (which see).

fireball, (s) n. See FAST BALL.

fireman, (s) n. A relief pitcher. He comes in to put out the "fire" (a rally by the opponents).

firing line, (s). The pitcher's plate and mound.

first, n. Short for first base.

first base. 1. The base to which the batter runs first, a 15″-square bag located diagonally to the right from home plate along the right field foul line, fixed exactly within the angle at the intersection of the line from home plate with the line from second base. Its outside edge coincides exactly with the outside edge of the foul line. The distance from the rear apex of home plate to its farthest edge is 90′. See BASE and diagram at the beginning of the rules. 2. The position designation of the player who habitually covers first base. Abbreviation: 1b.

first baseman. The player who habitually covers first base, therefore an infielder.

first division. The half of a league containing the teams with highest standing, such as the four leading teams in an eight-team league.

fitness of the ground. The condition of the field as affected by weather. The home team manager or captain decides on it before the game starts. Thereafter the umpire is sole judge, and he is likewise sole judge on beginning the second game of a double-header. See Rules 3.12, 3.13.

flag, (s) n. The pennant.

flipper, (s) n. 1. A pitcher. 2. His throwing arm.

floater, (s) n. A soft change-of-pace pitch with relatively little spin.

flutterball, (s) n. A slow wobbly pitch.

fly, n. See FLY BALL.

fly, v. To hit a fly ball that is caught. The batter "flies" or "flies out" to center field.

fly ball. A batted ball which rises an appreciable distance into the air. The term usually, though not invariably, applies to one that can be caught before it touches the ground, thus putting the batter out—therefore, in general, the opposite of a ground ball. A base-runner may not advance on a caught fly ball unless he is in contact with the base he was occupying when or after the fly ball is caught, or touched by the fielder. Should he be off that base when the ball is caught (whether it was fair or foul) he is out if a fielder secures the ball and touches the base before the runner can return to it. On the other hand he may advance (at his risk) on a caught foul fly if in contact with the base as previously specified. See Rules 2.26, 6.05(a), 7.08(d).

fly out. To be put out by hitting a caught fly ball. See FLY BALL.

fog, (s) v. To pitch a fast ball. The pitcher "fogs" one by the batter.

Forbes Field. Home grounds of the Pittsburgh Pirates. Distance from home plate to right field: 300′; center field: 457′; left field: 335′.

force, n. The situation that exists when a base-runner ceases to be entitled to a certain base and must reach the next one. Example: Batter hits a fair ground ball with a runner on first base. The runner, no longer entitled to first base, is "forced" to reach second base, and is "forced out" if a fielder, in possession of the ball, touches second base before the runner reaches it; tagging the runner is unnecessary. Actually the batter himself is forced to reach first base the instant he makes a fair hit since, at that instant, he automatically becomes a base-runner (which see). Therefore the common putout at first base (tagging unnecessary) is baseball's most frequent force play. A multiple force may exist. With all bases occupied, each of the three runners must reach the succeeding base. With first base unoccupied, however, no runners on second or third, or both second and third, are forced, since there is no runner on first base who is forced to advance. Furthermore, when a force situation exists it ceases if the batter

is put out at first base. A runner on first base may return to that base or he must be tagged if he attempts to reach second. A comparable situation obtains for any other previously-forced base-runners. No run scores if the third out is the result of a forceout. See Rules 2.27, 7.08(e).

force, v. To cause a putout resulting from a force situation. As the term is generally used, it is the batter who forces the runner, not the fielder making the putout.

force play. A play in which a base-runner is put out because of a force situation. See FORCE, n.

forceout, n. A putout occasioned by a force situation. See FORCE, n.

forfeiture, n. The awarding of the game, by a 9-0 score, to a team because of certain infractions by the opponents. Among the causes: delaying or shortening the game; disobeying an order for removal of a player (time limit: one minute); disobeying an order to condition the field; persistent rule violation; five or more minutes' avoidable delay in beginning a game after the umpire has called play; refusal to continue play unless play has been suspended or terminated by the umpire; refusal, after play has been legally suspended, to resume play within one minute after the umpire has called "Play!"; if a ground crew is unavailable to condition the field; if for any cause there are less than nine players on a team; if a team fails to begin the second game of a double-header within 20 minutes; if spectators interfere on the field and the field is not cleared within reasonable time (exacted against the home team). Only the umpire-in-chief may declare forfeiture. Should it occur after a regulation game (which see), all individual and team averages go into the records except that no pitcher may receive credit for a victory or be charged with a loss for that game. See Rules 2.28, 4.13, 4.14, 4.15.

fork ball. A pitched ball which is held at the top by the index and middle fingers, wide apart as possible, and at the bottom by the thumb. It acts like a knuckle ball (which see).

foul, adj. Not in fair territory. Outside of the foul lines. See FOUL BALL, FOUL GROUND, FOUL LINE.

foul, n. A foul ball (which see).

foul, v. To make a foul ball.

foul ball. A legally batted ball that settles on foul territory between home and first base or home and third base; one that bounds past first or third base on or over foul territory; one that, while on or over foul territory, touches the person of the umpire or a player, or any object foreign to the natural ground. The first and second uncaught foul balls in a time at bat count as strikes. Subsequent ones have no value with the exception of a foul bunt (which see). The batter may not advance to first on a foul ball, nor may a base-runner advance on any foul ball not caught. A foul ball caught on the fly retires the batter with certain exceptions for a foul tip (which see). On a caught foul ball a base-runner may advance—at his risk—if he tags up when or after the ball is caught. On an uncaught foul ball a base-runner must return to his base, but without liability of being put out. The ball is dead. See Rules 2.29, 5.09(e), 6.05(c).

foul bunt. A bunt which is a foul ball. It is an exception to the general rule on foul balls in that a foul bunt, when there are two strikes on the batter, puts him out, whether or not the ball is caught. See Rule 6.05(c).

foul ground. Any territory entirely *outside* the foul lines (the foul lines and foul poles being entirely in fair ground). See Rule 2.30. Also called foul territory.

foul line. A chalked line, not less than 3″ wide, extending from the home plate apex of the diamond to the boundary lines of the field—usually a fence or stand. At the top of the fence or stand the line must continue vertically at least 10′, usually in the form of a pole (foul pole). There are two foul lines formed by the right-angle apex at the rear of home plate. The first base, or right field, foul line extends diagonally to the right from home plate; first base is situated thereon 90′ from home base. The third base, or left field foul line, at right angles to the other line, extends diagonally to the left from home plate; third base is situated thereon 90′ from home base. *All* parts of the foul lines and the foul poles are in *fair* territory. The *outside* edge of the line is the dividing line. The foul lines are used to differentiate foul balls from fair balls, and serve to determine the base lines between home and first, and home and third, bases. See Rule 2.30 and diagram at the beginning of the rules.

foul out. To be put out by hitting a foul ball which is caught on the fly. See FOUL BALL.

foul pole. A pole which is a vertical continuation of the foul line (which see) above a fence or stand at the boundary of the field. It is entirely within fair territory. Major league rules decree it must be at least 10′ high.

foul strike. A foul ball not caught on the fly unless the batter has two strikes on him. Thereafter such a foul ball has no value. See FOUL BALL, FOUL TIP.

foul territory. See FOUL GROUND.

foul tip. A ball batted by the batter that goes sharp and direct from the bat to the catcher's hands and is legally caught. It is at all times a strike. Should it occur with two strikes on the batter, he is out. See Rule 2.31, 2.62(f).

four-bagger, (s) n. A home run.

four-master, (s) n. A home run.

four-ply wallop, (s) n. A home run.

frame, (s) n. An inning.

freak delivery. A term usually applied to illegal pitching deliveries rather than to merely unusual but legal deliveries like the knuckle ball or balloon ball. These freak deliveries would include the "mud ball," "emery ball," "shine ball," and "spitball." See Rule 8.02.

free ticket, (s). A base on balls. Also called "free trip."

front office, (s). The business office of a club.

full count. A count of three balls and two strikes on the batter (the highest possible).

full swing. A batting swing which is ruled a strike if the batter misses the ball. It is not precisely defined in the rules which merely define one type of strike as a pitched ball "struck at" by the batter and missed. A swing is sometimes started and halted. Umpires usually construe the intention to hit the ball proved when the batter "breaks" his wrists—snaps them in the completion of a swing—this bringing the bat around with a noticeable follow-through. A missed bunt, however, is also ruled a strike although no full swing takes place.

full wind-up. A wind-up habitually taken when there are no runners on base, thus distinguished from the shortened "stretch" used to prevent base-runners from taking too long a lead.

fungo, (s) n. A high fly. The term is usually applied to one hit in practice where the fungo-hitter tosses the ball a few feet into the air and then bats it, rather than a fly hit off a pitched ball.

fungo bat. A bat used for fungo-hitting. See FUNGO. It is thinner than the ordinary bat, with the weight centered more in the head.

G

game, n. 1. A contest between two teams. The game, ordinarily, is 9 full innings. But if the team second at bat has scored more runs in 8 innings than the team first at bat in 9 innings, the game is over, the former team winning. This also applies if the team last at bat in the 9th inning gains a lead at any time before three men are out. If the score is tied at the end of 9 full innings, extra innings are played, each team having equal innings at bat if necessary. Rain or other causes may dictate a legal game as short as 4½ or 5 innings. See REGULATION GAME and Rules 1.05, 4.10. 2. A unit of measurement to determine a league standing—meaning, in effect a won or lost game. If team A has won 57 and lost 33, and team B has won 54 and lost 36, then team A is 3 games ahead of team B—meaning that, should the two teams meet, team B would have to win 3 straight games to equalize the standing. Games may be gained or lost through intermediate opponents, and are even measured in "half" games. Team A would gain a half game on team B if team A beat team C while team B was idle. The following example shows how game margins are determined:

	Won	Lost
Team A	38	20
Team B	35	22

First: Subtract the figures in the Won column, giving a result of 3. Second: Subtract the figures in the Lost column, giving a result of 2. Third: Add these two results if the team having won the most games has lost the least; subtract them if the team having won the most has also lost the most (a possibility due to postponements). The former holds true in the example given, and, adding 3 and 2, the result is 5. Fourth: divide this result by 2. In this case team A leads team B by 2½ games.

garden, (s) n. The outfield. An outfielder is a "gardener."

gate, (s) n. The paid attendance.

get, v. To put an opponent out.

Giants. The New York team of the National League (major). An "Eastern" team.

glass arm, (s). A pitcher's arm susceptible to injury or affliction.

glove, n. An article to protect a fielder's hand when in the field, worn on the hand he does not throw with. That worn by all players save the catcher and first baseman is usually called a fielder's glove or mitt. It must be leather, not more than 12″ long nor 8″ wide from the base of the thumb crotch to the outside edge of the glove. Such gloves have fingers as well as a thumb.

FIELDER'S GLOVE

FIRST BASEMAN'S MITT
TRAPPER TYPE

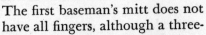

CATCHER'S MITT

The first baseman's mitt does not have all fingers, although a three-divisional "trapper's mitt" has been developed. It may not be longer than 12″ from top to bottom nor more than 8″ wide across the palm. Other rules limit webbing and spaces between thumb and finger section. The catcher's mitt is unrestricted but is almost invariably nearly round, heavily padded and with a depression ("hole" or "pocket") in the middle in which the ball will stick. For all details see Rules 1.16, 1.17, 1.18, 1.19.

go, (s) v. 1. To pitch. Jones is now "going" for the Sox. 2. To attempt to advance a base.

goat, (s) n. A player whose lapses cause his team's defeat or who performs poorly.

gone, (s) adj. Out. Two out: "two gone."

good, (s) adj. Pertaining to a pitch in the strike zone—particularly, near the heart of it.

good wood, (s). The thickest part ("fat part") of the bat where the ball can be most effectively hit—neither too near the tip or the handle.

goose egg, (s). A failure to score—so-called because the shape of the egg resembles the cipher (0).

gopher ball, (s). A pitch off which a home run is made. Like the gopher, which vanishes into its hole, the ball quickly vanishes into the stands or out of the park.

grand slam, (s). A home run with the bases full, also called "grandslammer."

Grapefruit League (s). A term applied to the series of practice games played by major (and high minor) league teams during the spring training season.

grass, n. A term that usually refers to the grassed part of the infield. When an infielder is playing "on the grass" he is playing in close to the plate, in front of the base path.

grass-cutter, (s) n. A hard hit ground ball.

Griffith Stadium. Home grounds of the Washington Senators. Distance from home plate to right field: 328′; center field: 420′; left field: 405′.

groove, (s) n. The strike zone, notably that near the center of the plate, waist-high. A straight pitch there is "in the groove."

groove, (s) v. To make a straight pitch over the plate in the strike zone.

ground ball. A batted ball which almost immediately hits the ground and bounces or rolls along the ground, thus one that cannot be caught on the fly. Commonly called "grounder."

grounder, (s) n. A ground ball.

ground out. To be thrown out at first base after hitting a ground ball at an infielder.

ground rule. A rule covering specific ground conditions in each park. The following rules are practically invariable in each park: Ball thrown into a stand, or bench, or over a fence: runner gets two bases; fair ball batted into spectators on field of play: two base hit for batter, and all runners advance two bases; fair ball batted into a stand less than 250′ from home plate: two bases (but major league rules specify there shall be no such stands); fair ball hitting the ground and then bouncing into a stand: two base hit. If a fly ball goes directly into a stand in fair territory or directly therein from a fielder's glove (or hand), not having hit the ground, it is a home run. See Rules 6.08 (e-i inc.), 7.05.

round rule double. A two base hit resulting from a ground rule. Most common: batted fair ball bouncing from the ground into

a stand; less common (in big league play): one hit into the spectators who are on the field of play. See GROUND RULE.

grounds, n. The area in which the game is played. See FITNESS OF THE GROUND.

guard, v. 1. To cover a base, in position to retire a runner if the opportunity presents. 2. To cover territory into which the ball may be batted. 3. To assume a batting stance so that the strike zone is guarded. Called "guarding the plate."

H

alf, n. A team's turn at bat in an inning. The visiting team bats in the first or "top" half, the home team in the last or "bottom" half.

all of Fame. A baseball "shrine" and museum in Cooperstown, N. Y., containing bronze plaques whereon are inscribed the names of great past players. There are also honor rolls of other individuals, managers, umpires, writers and executives who have made notable contributions to the game. One is elected to the Hall of Fame by a vote of prominent baseball writers.

ndcuff, (s) v. 1. To pitch extremely effectively, the batters being "handcuffed." 2. A term also used for the plight of a fielder who hesitates, in fielding a hard line drive, uncertain whether to put his glove up or down. The player is "frozen," and the drive "handcuffs" him.

ndle, v. To field a ball, the term usually applied to doing so suc-

cessfully. The shortstop handles seven chances.

handle hit. A hit made off the handle of the bat.

hang, (s) v. A term applied to the action of a curve ball which fails to break.

heave-ho, (s) n. Removal from the game. The umpire gives a player the "heave-ho."

heaver, (s) n. A pitcher.

hickory, (s) n. A bat (although most good bats are of ash).

hidden ball. A ruse in which a baseman conceals the ball, and attempts to catch the runner off the base, should the latter believe the pitcher has it.

high, adj. Pertaining to a pitched ball above the batter's shoulders. Sometimes also applied to one in the strike zone, but relatively high up in it—around the chest.

hill, (s) n. The pitcher's mound (which see).

hit, v. 1. To make a base hit. 2. To take a turn at bat—whether or not the ball is actually hit.

hit, n. A term which, by itself, denotes a base hit. Abbreviation: h. See FAIR BALL and BASE HIT.

hit-and-run, n. A maneuver in which the batter and base-runner coordinate. At the pitch, the runner on first starts for second base in an attempt to draw the second baseman or shortstop from his customary position wide of second base. The fielder runs to second base to cover the throw from the catcher to stop an apparently-attempted stolen base. The batter then must try to hit the ball through the spot the fielder has vacated. A variation is the run-and-hit (which see).

hit batter. A batter hit by a pitched ball. He is entitled to first base and not charged with a time at bat, provided he does not swing at it, and provided he makes a reasonable effort to get out of its way. The ball is then dead. If he fails to try to avoid being hit, the umpire calls "ball" or "strike" as the case may be. See Rule 6.07(b).

hitter, n. The batter.

hit the dirt, (s). To slide.

hitting, n. Batting.

hold, v. To fail to make an attempt to advance. The runner holds his base. The term is likewise used when no, or little, lead is taken. The runner holds—and sometimes he is held by the baseman who plays close to it.

hole, n. A spot not covered by a fielder. The batter singles through a hole between first and second. See also IN THE HOLE.

Hollywood Stars. The Hollywood team of the Pacific Coast League (AAA). A "Southern" team.

home, n. 1. Short for home plate. 2. Home grounds.

home plate. A five-sided white rubber slab set level with the base lines, and located at the rear apex of the diamond, sometimes called "home base." Its rear apex is a right angle which determines the foul lines. The sides of the plate itself, formed by this angle, are 12″ long. At these two points the next two sides of the plate continue for a distance of 8½′ parallel to an imaginary line between home plate and second base. The extremities of these lines are connected with a line 17″ long—the fifth side of the base which is accordingly parallel to an imaginary line between first and third base. See inset in the diagram at the beginning of the rules. In major league play home plate must be at least 60′ from any stand or fence in foul territory, 250′ in fair territory. It is 90′ away from both first and third base; 60′ 6″ from the pitcher's plate; 127′ 3⅜″ from second base. The batter stands roughly opposite home plate within the batter's box. The pitcher must pitch the ball over home plate within the strike zone in order to record a strike, and a base-runner must safely reach home plate after touching the other bases in order to score a run. Therefore both in location and importance home plate is, in effect, the head of the field and of the game. See Rule 1.09.

homer, (s) n. A home run.

home run. A safe hit where, without benefit of an error, the batter completes the circuit of the bases and scores a run. In major league play the most common type is a fair ball batted outside the regular playing field, a run automatically awarded the player as soon as he jogs around the bases. A batted fly ball is judged fair or foul by where it passes outside the playing field. Should a stand in fair territory be less than 250′ from the plate (never true in major league play), only a two base hit is awarded. The same applies to a fair ball that strikes the ground and bounds over a fence, to any fair ball deflected by a fielder into a stand in foul territory, and a fair *ground* ball deflected by him into a stand in fair territory. A *fly* ball directly deflected by a fielder into a stand in fair territory is a home run, however. A less common type of home run is the inside-the-park home run where the player does not score automatically. He must beat the ball to home plate, scoring if untagged. Abbreviation: HR. See Rules 6.08(e, i), 7.05(a).

home team. The team on whose grounds the game is played, and which bats last. If a game is played on neutral grounds, the home team is designated by mutual agreement. See Rules 2.33 and 4.02.

hook, (s) n. A curve ball.

hook slide. A slide in which the runner slides feet-first, veering his body away from the bag so that only his trailing foot will touch or hook the base. Purpose: To give the baseman less target to tag. Also called fall-away slide.

hop, n. 1. The slight upward rise of a fast ball pitch. 2. The bounding action of a ground ball. The fielder grabs it on the second "hop."

horse-collar, (s) n. 1. Failure to score. So called because the shape of a cipher (0) resembles that of a horse-collar. 2. Failure by a batter to secure a safe hit during a game.

horse-collar, (s) v. 1. To hold the opponents scoreless. 2. To prevent a given batter from hitting safely during a game.

horsehide, (s) n. The ball.

hot corner, (s). Third base.

hot stove league, (s). An off-season gathering of fans who discuss baseball. It derives from rural gatherings, often around a heating stove in a small store, where fans hash over the past and future of the game.

hug, (s) v. 1. To stay close to a base. 2. To take a batting stance close to the plate.

hurl, (s) v. To pitch.

hurler, (s) n. A pitcher.

I

illegal, adj. Contrary to the rules.

illegally batted ball. A ball batted when either of the batter's feet is outside the lines of the bat-

ter's box when he hits the ball. The batter is out, and the ball is dead, any runners returning to their bases. The same applies if the batter intentionally hits the ball a second time. See Rules 6.05 (g), 6.06(b).

illegal pitch. A pitch delivered to the batter when the pitcher is not in pitching position, i.e., his pivot foot not in contact with the pitcher's plate. It is a balk if there is anyone on base, otherwise a ball, provided the batter does not strike at it. If, with the bases unoccupied, the batter hits an illegal pitch and reaches first, the play counts. It is not ruled a "ball." See Rules 2.35, 8.01(d), 8.05(e).

in, adv. 1. Toward or near the home plate from the field. A fielder plays "in," perhaps expecting a bunt. 2. In the strike zone. The pitcher puts one "in" or "in there."

incurve, n. A curve, delivered by a right-handed pitcher, that curves toward a right-handed batter, or the same for left-handers. Also called inshoot. However, the term "screwball" is more common in modern times.

Indianapolis Indians. The Indianapolis team of the American Association (AAA). An "Eastern" team.

Indians. The Cleveland team of the American League (major). A "Western" team. Also the Indianapolis team of the American Association (AAA). An "Eastern" team. Also the Seattle team of the Pacific Coast League (AAA). A "Northern" team.

infield, n. The diamond proper, including the four bases and all territory within, including the base paths. There is no actual specified dividing line between the infield and outfield, but the former term commonly designates that territory covered by infielders. See Rule 2.36.

infielder, n. A fielder who habitually covers an infield position, notably the first, second and third basemen and the shortstop. The pitcher and catcher cover infield positions, but are commonly called the battery, rather than infielders. Abbreviation: if.

infield-fly, n. A term specifically applied to a situation when, before there are two out, while first and second, or first, second and third bases are occupied, the batter hits a fair fly ball, other than a line drive, or a fly in attempting to bunt, that can reasonably be caught by an infielder or an outfielder in an infield position. In that case the umpire declares it an infield-fly, and the batter is automatically out. The runners are *not* forced to advance, regardless of whether or not the ball is subsequently caught, and they may attempt to advance at the risk of its being caught. By removing the force situation, the rule prevents *two* men on base from being doubled up if the fielder should purposely let the ball drop in order to force two non-advancing runners. It is not necessary with only a runner on first. See Rule 2.37.

infield hit. A base hit (which see) resulting from a ball that does not go out of the infield.

in flight. Pertaining to a batted, thrown, or pitched ball which has not yet touched the ground or some other object other than a fielder. See Rule 2.38.

initial sack, (s). First base.

in jeopardy. A term indicating that the ball is in play and an offensive player may be put out. See Rule 2.39.

inning, n. A division of the game, dictated by the number of the batting team retired. It is divided into two halves. In the first half the visiting team bats; in the second half the home team does so. A half-inning lasts until three men are put out (except when the team batting last gains the lead in a ninth or extra inning), after which that team takes the field, and the other team bats. A normal game consists of nine innings. See GAME and REGULATION GAME for exceptions. See Rule 2.40.

in order, (s). The retirement of the first three batters in an inning. The side is out "in order."

in play. The situation when the ball is not dead, and whatever happens comprises the actual progress of the game. The ball is in play or "alive" after being a dead ball when it is held by the pitcher standing in his position, and the umpire has called "Play!" See Rules 5.07, 5.09, 5.10.

inshoot, n. See INCURVE.

inside, adj. Near the batter. An inside pitch is one that comes between him and the home plate or that crosses the plate on the side nearest him.

inside baseball, (s). Smart strategic baseball. Not to be confused with *indoor* baseball from which softball derived.

insurance, (s) n. The amassing of a sufficient lead so that an opposing rally would not reasonably be expected to wipe it out. Often called "run insurance."

intentional pass. A base on balls intentionally issued. Reasons include: to avoid pitching to a dangerous batter to get at a weaker one; to get at a right-handed batter (if pitcher is right-handed) or left-handed batter for left-handed pitcher; to set up a possible double play or force play, should first base be unoccupied, by putting a runner on first and establishing a force situation.

intercept, v. To make a cut-off (which see).

interference, n. Obstruction of the regular course of play. This may be by a fielder, batter, base-runner, umpire, coacher or person not in the game. Penalties vary (sometimes there are none), and the rules are complicated. It may be stated, in general, that the ball is dead when a fielder or batter is interfered with. See INTERFERENCE and OBSTRUCTION in the playing rules index, which terms give applicable rule numbers for the specific type.

intermission, n. A term usually applied in baseball to the time between games of a double-header. Twenty minutes is standard, although it may be shortened or lengthened due to weather conditions. The time between half-innings is, in a sense, an intermission. Here players are allowed a reasonable time to take or return from the field.

International League. An AAA minor league consisting of the Baltimore Orioles, Buffalo Bisons, Jersey City Little Giants, Montreal Royals, Rochester Red Wings, Springfield Cubs, Syracuse Chiefs, and Toronto Maple Leafs. The other two AAA leagues are the American Association and the Pacific Coast League.

J

jackpot, (s) n. A home run with the bases full.

jersey, n. A light wool long-sleeved garment often worn under the shirt. See UNIFORM.

Jersey City Little Giants. The Jersey City team of the International League (AAA). A "Southern" team.

jockey, (s) n. One who "rides" the opposing players, i.e., heckles them. Often called "bench jockey."

K

kalsomine, (s) v. To hold the opponents scoreless. To shut out or "whitewash."

Kansas City Blues. The Kansas City (Mo.) team of the American Association (AAA). A "Western" team.

keystone, (s) n. Second base, often called the "keystone sack." The second baseman and shortstop are the "keystone combination."

kick, (s) v. 1. To "boot" the ball with the foot or make a bad infield error. 2. To protest.

in the hole, (s). 1. Having an unfavorable count when pitching or batting. With a count of 3 balls and no strikes, the pitcher is in the hole. With a count of 2 strikes and no balls, the batter is in the hole. 2. The status of the player who is two turns away from batting, and who therefore follows the man "on deck."

iron man, (s). A durable player.

ivory, (s) n. A term applied to professional baseball players. Scouts in search of promising players are styled "ivory-hunters."

jockey, (s) v. To heckle the opponents.

juggle, (s) v. To mis-handle a ball (by a fielder). He may not actually drop it, but may consume so much time that the opposing runner is safe.

jug-handled curve, (s). A wide sweeping curve.

Junior World Series. A term sometimes applied to the Little World Series (which see).

jump, (s) n. A hop on a pitched ball. See HOP.

knock down, (s). To pitch so close to a batter that he falls to the ground to avoid the ball. In baseball the term does *not* imply actually hitting him.

knock out, (s). To bat so effectively that the pitcher must be removed. He is "knocked out of the box."

knuckle ball. A pitched ball in which the surface is held against the knuckles of the first two fingers (sometimes also the third)

This gives it less than normal spin, and causes it to wobble to some extent and to drop sud-

denly near the plate. Often called "knuckler."

knuckler, (s) n. See KNUCKLE BALL.

L

ladies' day. A day when ladies are admitted free.

lay one down, (s). To bunt.

lead, (s) v. 1. To station one's self off base (by a base-runner) in the direction of the next base, in order to have less ground to cover if an advance is attempted. 2. To be ahead in the score.

lead-off, n. 1. The first player in the batting order. 2. The first player to bat in a given inning.

league, n. A group of clubs which play a common schedule to decide a championship. Most baseball leagues contain eight clubs. See MAJOR LEAGUE, MINOR LEAGUE and accompanying cross-references.

leather, (s) n. A baseball.

left field. 1. The outfield territory beyond third base, within the left field foul line (continuation of third base foul line) and extending to that territory beyond second base which is covered by the center fielder. 2. The name of the position occupied by the player who covers left field. Abbreviation: lf.

left fielder. An outfielder who is assigned to cover left field territory.

leftie, (s) n. A left-handed player, notably one who throws left-handed.

left on base. The number of base-runners still on base when an inning ends. Example: If, with two out and three men on base, the batter strikes out, there are three men left on base. Sometimes what would appear to be the batter is left on base. See BASE-RUNNER and Rule 6.08, and note that the batter becomes a base-runner *instantly* when he makes a fair hit, *not* merely when he reaches first base safely.

legal, adj. In accordance with the rules.

length, (s) n. The margin of games in the standing. A team 5 games ahead is 5 "lengths" ahead.

letter-high, adj. Pertaining to a pitch that comes to the batter chest-high, hence abreast that part of his uniform bearing the lettering of his club.

let-up pitch. A pitch of less than full speed. A change of pace.

life, (s) n. Another chance or a reprieve for the batting team, as when the batter reaches first on an error or a fielder fails to catch a foul fly he hits.

line, n. See BASE LINE, FOUL LINE.

line, v. 1. To hit a line drive. 2. To put lines on the field, such as foul lines, box lines.

line drive. A solidly hit ball, most of whose flight approximately parallels the ground.

line out. To hit a line drive which is caught on the fly, putting the batter out.

liner, n. See LINE DRIVE.

line-up, n. The positions, designated by the manager or captain, which team members will play. The batting order is an integral part of the line-up. See BATTING ORDER.

Little Giants. The Jersey City team of the International League (AAA). A "Southern" team.

Little World Series. A four-out-of-seven series between the winners of the Shaughnessy Play-offs in the American Association and International Leagues (both AAA). See SHAUGHNESSY PLAY-OFFS.

live ball. A ball in play.

loaded, (s) adj. Bases full.

long ball. A ball batted deep to the outfield or over a fence. A powerful batter is a "long ball hitter."

look at, (s). To fail to swing at a pitched ball (by the batter).

loop, (s) n. A league or conference.

loose, (s) adj. 1. Pertaining to a ball not in possession of a fielder, notably one muffed, that gets by him or the result of a wild throw. 2. Inept or sloppy fielding or pitching.

Los Angeles Angels. The Los Angeles team of the Pacific Coast League (AAA). A "Southern" team.

losing pitcher. A term not rigidly standardized, but usually determined by the following rules: A pitcher: 1. who starts and completes a losing game; 2. who comes in on relief with his team ahead or tied and then completes a losing game; 3. who comes in on relief with his team ahead or tied and then leaves the game with a deficit that is not subsequently cancelled or overcome; 4. who starts a game and then leaves it with a deficit that is not subsequently cancelled or overcome. However, a losing pitcher is not charged for runs scored by runners who got on against a preceding pitcher, nor is he charged for the first batter he faces if he enters with a ball-and-strike deficit given up by the preceding pitcher (2 or 3 balls and 1 or 0 strikes, or 3 balls and 2 strikes). See Rules 10.15 (f & g), 10.16.

Louisville Colonels. The Louisville team of the American Association (AAA). An "Eastern" team.

lower half. The last or bottom half of an inning.

lumber, (s) n. A bat.

M

mace, (s) n. A bat.

major league. The highest-ranking leagues. There are two major leagues, the American League and the National League, (both of which see).

manage, v. To act as manager.

manager, n. A term applied in professional baseball to the man who runs the team. He selects line-ups, formulates plays, decides on strategy and tactics and often coaches. He also usually has an important part in the buying selling and trading of players. The manager may also play, in which case he is a playing manager. In amateur or semi-professional baseball, the manager may be subservient to a coach—the manager's duties concerned more with scheduling, caring for equipment, etc.

Maple Leafs. The Toronto team of the International League (AAA). A "Northern" team.

marathon, (s) n. A long extra-inning game.

marker, (s) n. A run.

mascot, n. A term usually applied in professional baseball to a youth who tends to player's equipment and does odd chores. Often the bat boy.

MASK

mask, n. A protective device to shield the face of the catcher and the plate umpire against injury, particularly from line fouls from the bat. Not mandatory in the rules, but invariably worn (save by occasional small boys who don't mind courting disaster).

meat hand, (s). The hand not wearing a glove.

Millers. The Minneapolis team of the American Association (AAA). A "Western" team.

Milwaukee Brewers. The Milwaukee team of the American Association (AAA). A "Western" team.

nail, (s) v. To put out a runner at a base.

nap, (s) v. To fail to be alert. A runner caught off base is "caught napping."

Minneapolis Millers. The Minneapolis team of the American Association (AAA). A "Western" team.

minor league. A term applied to any professional league except the two major leagues (American and National). There are over 60 in the Western Hemisphere, most of them in the United States. (See AAA, AA, A, B, C, D).

miscue, (s) n. An error.

miscue, (s) v. To make an error.

mix up, (s). To employ a variety of pitches when pitching.

money player, (s). One who habitually comes through in the pinch.

Montreal Royals. The Montreal team of the International League (AAA). A "Northern" team.

mound, n. The mound in which the pitcher's plate is set. It is 15″ above the rest of the field. See Rule 1.09.

moundsman, (s). A pitcher.

move up, (s). To advance a base.

mud ball, (s). A ball on which mud has been rubbed. It is illegal to apply foreign substance to the ball.

Mud Hens (or Mudhens). The Toledo team of the American Association (AAA). An "Eastern" team.

muff, v. To drop a ball, notably when an error results.

N

National Association of Professional Baseball Leagues. The governing body of minor league baseball in the United States, as well as a few other leagues in the Western

Hemisphere. Often called National Association for short. See MINOR LEAGUE.

National Baseball Congress. An organization governing a large portion of semi-professional baseball.

national game. A term commonly applied in the United States to baseball.

National League. One of the two major leagues (the other is the American), consisting of the Boston Braves, Brooklyn Dodgers, Chicago Cubs, Cincinnati Reds, New York Giants, Philadelphia Phillies, Pittsburgh Pirates and St. Louis Cardinals.

Nationals, (s). A nickname for the Washington Senators.

Nats, (s). Short for Nationals (Washington Senators).

New York Giants. A major league team, being an "Eastern" one in the National League. Home grounds: The Polo Grounds.

New York Yankees. A major league team, being an "Eastern" one in the American League. Home grounds: Yankee Stadium.

nightcap, (s) n. The second game of a double-header.

night game. A game played at night, under artificial lights. The night game is practically the invariable rule in modern minor league play, and is of considerable popularity in the majors.

nine, n. A baseball team.

nip, (s) v. To retire a base-runner on a close play.

no-hit no-run. A game in which a pitcher wins the game and permits his opponents no base hits and no runs, hence a rare feat. For it to be recognized as a notable accomplishment, the game must go nine or more innings.

no-hitter, (s). See NO-HIT NO-RUN.

Northern team. A team classified as "Northern" in certain leagues for scheduling purposes, such as the Pacific Coast and International Leagues. In the Pacific Coast League the four Northern teams are the Oakland Oaks, Portland Beavers, San Francisco Seals and Seattle Indians. International League: Buffalo Bisons, Montreal Royals, Rochester Red Wings and Toronto Maple Leafs.

numbering, n. A system whereby identification numbers are put on the backs of uniforms. Major league rules do not make this obligatory, but the practice is practically universal throughout modern baseball.

O

Oakland Oaks. The Oakland team of the Pacific Coast League (AAA). A "Northern" team.

Oaks. The Oakland Oaks.

obstruction, n. A term applied to certain types of bodily interference, by a fielder, or, in certain cases, by the batter. See INTERFERENCE and also listings under OBSTRUCTION and INTERFERENCE in the Rules index. Particularly 7.04(c), 7.06 (a & b).

on base. The status of a base-runner occupying a base.

on deck. About to bat next. The "on deck" man often occupies the batter's circle.

one old cat, (s). A type of rounders (which see) in which there is only one batter and one base besides home plate. The batter must run to the base and return to the plate or else be forced out. When he is out, the rotation principle is the same as in rounders, and when a player catches a fly ball, he exchanges places with the batter. It can be played with as few as three or four fielders. Should there be more than that available, "two old cat" or "three old cat" will probably be played. See those terms.

one-two-three, (s). See IN ORDER.

open stance. A batting stance in which the left foot is pulled back from an imaginary line between the pitcher's plate and home plate (for a right-handed batter). Right foot for a left-handed batter.

Orioles. The Baltimore team of the International League (AAA). A "Southern" team.

out, adj. The status of a batter or base-runner who is retired (put out) by the fielding side. A team's turn at bat (a half inning) continues until 3 of its players are out. Among the causes of an out: strikeout; batting out of turn; stepping out of the batter's box; hitting a ball that is caught on the .fly; an infield-fly under certain circumstances; batting the ball twice; being tagged by the ball when off base when the ball is in play; being forced; running outside the three-foot line or the base line, except to avoid a player who is fielding the ball; being hit by a batted ball; failure to return to a base before the ball is returned there after a batted ball is caught on the fly; failure to touch a base, provided the ball is returned there or the runner is tagged with it before he can return; passing a preceding baserunner; certain rule breaches by teammates or coaches. See STRIKEOUT, FORCE, TAG, DOUBLE PLAY, DOUBLED UP, FLY BALL, INFIELD-FLY. The above list covers most, but not all situations which make a player out. The most common are the force, particularly where the batter, having become a base-runner, is thrown out at first base; the caught fly ball; the strikeout; the tag. See Rule 2.46.

out, n. That which occurs when a player is put out. The abbreviation is po. (for putout) credited to the fielder who makes it. See Rule 2.46.

outcurve, n. A curve, delivered by a right-handed pitcher, that curves away from a right-handed batter (or left-handed in both instances). The most common curve. One curving out and down is an outdrop.

outfield, n. The extensive grassed territory beyond the infield and usually bounded by fences or stands. There is no actual dividing line between the outfield and infield specified in the rules, but the term commonly designates territory covered by the three outfielders. A ball batted into the outfield, unless caught on the fly, almost invariably results in a hit for one or more bases.

outfielder, n. A fielder who habitually covers an outfield position. See Rule 2.47. There are three: left fielder, center fielder, right fielder. Their positions, guided chiefly by the habits of the batter, may vary by considerable distances both from home plate and to right or left. Abbreviation: of.

out in order. The situation when the first three batters in an inning are all retired, none reaching first base.

outlaw, (s) n. A player banned from playing in organized baseball.

outside, adj. Away from the batter. An outside pitch is one that misses the opposite side of the plate from him or crosses the plate on the side farthest from him.

over-run, v. To run past a base and thus endanger one's self of being tagged out. It is, however, permissible to over-run first base if it is returned to immediately. See Rule 6.08(j).

over-slide, v. To slide beyond a base with same liabilities as to over-run. Should a runner, attempting to steal, be tagged out after over-sliding a base, he is not credited with a stolen base. See Rules 2.48, 6.08(j), 10.11(b).

overtime, (s) n. Any inning after the ninth.

P

pace-setter, (s) n. The leading team in a league, or leading player in batting averages, home runs, etc.

Pacific Coast League. An AAA minor league consisting of the Hollywood Stars, Los Angeles Angels, Oakland Oaks, Portland Beavers, Sacramento Senators, San Diego Padres, San Francisco Seals and Seattle Indians. The other two AAA leagues are the American Association and International League.

Padres. The San Diego team of the Pacific Coast League (AAA). A "Southern" team.

Pale Hose, (s). A nickname for the Chicago White Sox.

parallel stance. See SQUARE STANCE.

park, n. A baseball field, including its seating arrangements.

park, (s) v. To hit a ball into the stands. It is "parked" there.

pass, n. 1. A base on balls. 2. A free admission.

pass, v. To give up a base on balls.

passed ball. A misplay, charged to the catcher, when a base-runner advances by the catcher's failure to hold or control a legally pitched ball that should have been held or controlled with ordinary effort. It is not charged as an error unless the batter reaches first base because of a dropped third strike. Abbreviation: PB. See Rules 10.10(b), 10.12(b).

pennant, n. A flag awarded a club winning a league championship. As commonly used the term refers more to the honor, title and monetary advantages than to the actual piece of bunting itself.

pepper game, (s). Brisk pre-game practice consisting of short quick throws and bunts in rapid succession.

percentage, n. 1. A system used to determine standings and averages, usually carried out to three decimal points. A team having won 75 games and lost 25 has a percentage of .750. Abbreviation: PC. 2. A term used to denote the law of probabilities. A team "plays percentage" when it attempts a maneuver most likely to succeed from probabilities, such as intentionally walking a batter to create a force possibility in certain situations.

perfect game. A no-hit no-run game in which no player reaches first base for any cause whatsoever—an exceedingly rare pitching performance. To be recognized as noteworthy, the feat must be for nine or more innings.

person, n. Any part of a player or umpire's body, his clothing or his equipment.

Philadelphia Athletics. A major league team, being an "Eastern" one in the American League. Home grounds: Shibe Park.

Philadelphia Phillies. A major league team, being an "Eastern" one in the National League. Home grounds: Shibe Park.

Phillies. The Philadelphia Phillies.

Phils, (s). A nickname for the Phillies.

pick off. To catch a runner off base, usually by a sudden throw from the pitcher or catcher.

pick-up, n. A low throw which the fielder catches just after it bounces up from the ground—often made by a first baseman on an infielder's low throw.

pilfer, (s) v. To steal a base.

pinch, (s) n. A desperate situation, such as a team's last out when it is trailing.

pinch hitter. A batter who is inserted into the batting order to bat for another batter—often in the pinch. Should he remain in the game after batting, he takes the place in the batting order of the batter displaced. See BATTING ORDER and Rules 3.04, 3.05.

pinch runner. A player selected to run for a teammate who has reached a base. The original base-runner cannot continue in the game. See Rules 3.04, 3.05.

Pirates. The Pittsburgh team of the National League (major). A "Western" team.

pitch, n. A ball delivered to the batter by the pitcher. The term applies to the delivery's legality, type, speed, accuracy. See PITCHING, BALL, 2, STRIKE, STRIKEOUT, ILLEGAL PITCH, BALK, SET POSITION, WINDUP POSITION, WILD PITCH, CURVE, DROP, FLOATER, FAST BALL, CHANGE OF PACE and Rules 2.51, 8.01-8.06, inclusive.

pitch, v. To deliver the ball to the home plate when in contact with the pitcher's plate and acting in the capacity of pitcher. See PITCH, n. and PITCHING.

pitcher, n. The defensive player designated to deliver the pitch to the batter. His primary objective is to put out the batter, either by striking him out or causing him to hit the ball ineffectually. The starting pitcher must pitch until the first batter has completed his turn at bat. A relief pitcher must pitch to the batter at bat until that batter has completed his turn at bat or until the side has been retired. The pitcher is considered the most important member of the team, since an unusually effective one can virtually dominate the game by retiring opposing batters. The position is so strenuous that a pitcher normally requires two or three days' rest between games. Abbreviation: p. See PITCH, n., PITCHING, STARTING PITCHER, RELIEF PITCHER, WINNING PITCHER, LOSING PITCHER and Rules 2.52, 3.06, 3.07, 8.01-8.06 inclusive.

pitcher's box. A term commonly applied to the territory in which the pitcher stands. See PITCHER'S MOUND and PITCHER'S PLATE.

pitcher's duel. A close, low-scoring game dominated by the pitchers.

pitcher's mound. The mound in which the pitcher's plate is set. It is 15″ above the level of the ground at home base and the base lines, and it must slope down gradually to these points. See Rule 1.09 and inset diagram at the beginning of the rules.

pitcher's plate. A white rubber slab 24″ long and 6″ wide, level with the ground surface on the pitcher's mound, and located 60′ 6″ from home base on a direct line between home base and second base, its long axis at right angles to this line. Often called the "rubber." See Rule 1.09 and diagram at the beginning of the rules.

pitcher's rubber. See PITCHER'S PLATE.

pitching, n. The delivery of the ball to the batter by the pitcher. Preliminary to pitching he must take his position facing the batter with his pivot foot (which see) always on or in front of and in contact with the pitcher's plate. In delivering the ball to the batter, his other foot is free, except that he cannot step to either side of the pitcher's plate. He may not raise either foot until in the act of delivering the ball to the batter, or in throwing to a base. He may apply no foreign substance to the ball, may not spit on the ball or his glove, may not rub the ball on his glove, person or clothing, and may not deface the ball in any manner. He may, however, use powdered resin to dry his hands. When the batter is in his proper position he may not throw the ball to any player save the catcher except in attempting to retire a base-runner. He is penalized for a balk (which see). The style of throwing is not restricted. It may be overhand, sidearm or underhand, but the first two are most common. Many pertinent cross-references to pitching are listed under PITCH, n. and PITCHER. The pitching rules are Rules 8.01-8.06 inclusive.

pitching staff. The total number of pitchers possessed by a club or squad.

pitch-out, n. A deliberately wide pitch which the batter cannot hit. Among motives: to thwart an attempted hit-and-run, squeeze or steal.

Pittsburgh Pirates. A major league team, being a "Western" one in the National League. Home grounds: Forbes Field.

pivot, n. One who pivots. See also PIVOT FOOT.

pivot, v. To act as an intermediary, notably in relaying a ball. Example: With a runner on first base, the ball is hit to the shortstop. He tosses the ball to the second baseman who touches second base, pivots (turns), and throws it to first base for a double play. The second baseman is the "pivot man."

pivot foot. The foot in contact with the pitcher's plate in pitching. It acts as the pitcher's base of support, and is hence the opposite of the one with which he steps forward. A right-handed pitcher's pivot foot is the right one, since he steps forward with the left foot. See Rules 2.53, 8.01.

plate, n. A term commonly applied to home plate (which see).

plate umpire. The umpire who works behind home plate. See UMPIRE-IN-CHIEF.

platter, (s) n. Home plate.

play, n. A term commonly applied in baseball to any specific action which takes place between one pitch and the next one—such as a putout, double play, error, stolen base, etc.

"Play!" The command of the umpire to start or resume the game.

play-by-play. n. A description of a game, giving full details. It may be a broadcast, telecast or newspaper write-up.

playing manager. A manager who likewise plays a position on the team.

play-off, n. An extra game or series to break a tie in the standings or one dictated by league rules to decide league winners. In the major leagues, if teams are tied at the end of the season, there is a one-game play-off in the American League, a two-out-of-three game play-off in the National League. Minor leagues commonly use a play-off system involving the four leading teams. See SHAUGHNESSY PLAY-OFFS. It should be noted that this type of play-off is not one caused by a tie. The World Series (which see) may also be considered a type of play-off.

pocket, n. The part of the glove or mitt into which the ball normally fits, sometimes created or improved by manipulating or pounding the glove—"breaking it in."

pole, (s) v. To bat a ball hard. The batter "poles" a triple.

Polo Grounds. Home grounds of the New York Giants. Distance from home plate to right field: 258'; center field: 505'; left field: 279'.

pop, (s) v. To bat a short high fly, fair or foul, which can be easily caught. Also called "pop-up."

pop fly, (s). A short high fly which can be easily caught.

pop-up (s) n. A pop fly.

pop up, (s). To make a pop-up.

Portland Beavers. The Portland (Oregon) team of the Pacific Coast League (AAA). A "Northern" team.

port-sider, (s) n. A left-handed thrower, notably a pitcher.

powder, (s) v. To bat a ball hard.

pro, (s) n. A professional. In baseball the term more specifically denotes an experienced reliable player apt to come through in the pinch.

protest, n. A complaint, either unofficial or official. Rules specify that unofficial protests on the umpire's judgment and decision on a play are forbidden, but most umpires usually countenance a certain amount of "squawking" if it is not overdone. An official protest may not be made on the umpire's judgment of fact, as to whether a pitch is a strike or a ball, a runner out or safe, etc. However, should the decision be based on a faulty interpretation of a rule, the protest may be sustained. See Rules 4.16, 9.04.

pull, v. To swing early at the ball when batting. When a right-handed batter "pulls" the ball he hits it in the direction of third base and left field, and one who does so consistently is a "pull hitter." First base and right field

for a left-handed batter. The opposite of slicing.

pull off (s). 1. To lure a base-runner off his base by any legal ruse. 2. To accomplish. A team "pulls off" a double steal.

pull out of the fire, (s). To win a game that seemed irretrievably lost.

pull the string, (s). To deliver a change of pace—a ball slower than a fast ball, but made with the same motion in an effort to fool the batter.

pump, (s) v. To take a full windup when pitching. See WINDUP.

put out. To retire a base-runner or a batter. To make a putout. (See PUTOUT.)

putout, n. The action of a defensive player in retiring (putting out) an opponent. In the scoring records the number he makes is credited to a player, and the abbreviation is po. The most common putouts are credited to a fielder catching a fly ball, to a player making a tag or force play, to the catcher when the batter strikes out. Others, more complicated, are listed under Rule 10.07.

Q

quick return. A quick, sudden pitch calculated to take advantage of the batter when he is off balance

from a previous pitch. It is illegal. See Rule 8.02(d).

R

rabbit ball, (s). A term applied to the modern baseball, believed to be livelier than that of an earlier era. This is controversial.

rabbit-ears, (s) n. A player who is unduly sensitive to taunts ("riding") by the opponents.

rainbow, (s). See BALLOON BALL.

raincheck, n. A ticket stub issued to spectators. If a single game, or first game of a double-header, fails to become a regulation game (4½ or 5 innings) because of rain or other causes, the stub admits the holder free to any subsequent regular-season game in the park where issued. See REGULATION GAME.

rained out. Postponed or canceled because of rain.

rally, n. A scoring surge.

receive, v. To play the position of catcher.

receiver, n. The catcher.

recruit, n. A new or inexperienced player, notably one who has not played in a league of as high a caliber.

Red Birds. The Columbus team of the American Association (AAA). An "Eastern" team. Also a nickname for the St. Louis Cardinals, usually run together: "Redbirds."

Reds. The Cincinnati team of the National League (major). A "Western" team.

Red Sox. The Boston team of the American League (major). An "Eastern" team.

Red Wings. The Rochester team of the International League (AAA). A "Northern" team. .

regulation game. Any game which becomes an official game (whether won or tied) and where the players' performances go into the records (and which invalidates a raincheck). Not only the normal 9 or 8½-inning game is a regulation game. If called, due to weather conditions, darkness or other causes, it is a regulation game provided 5 or more equal innings have been played; or if the team second at bat shall have made more runs at the end of its 4th inning, or before the completion of its 5th inning, than the team first at bat has made in 5 completed innings. This, therefore, applies to any game beyond this point, whether 6, 9, 15 innings or whatever. Should a tie result, under these regulations, it is a regulation drawn game. If the game does not go 4½ or 5 innings by these regulations, it is simply "no game" whether the score is tied or not. See GAME, TIE and Rules 2.55, 4.10, 4.11.

relay, v. To receive the ball from one player and throw it to another.

release, v. To drop a player from the roster rather than trading him or selling him.

relief pitcher. A pitcher who comes into the game in place of another. When he does so he is not charged, in the scoring records, for men already on base or for the batter if the batter enjoys an advantage in balls and strikes at this point, i.e., if such base-runners or the batter subsequently score, this will not affect his earned run average or his status as a losing pitcher. A relief pitcher must pitch until the first batter he faces has completed his turn at bat, or the side has been put out, barring incapacitating injury or illness. The term "relief pitcher" is also applied to a pitcher who is habitually used for relief work, as contrasted to one given regular starting assignments. See EARNED RUN, LOSING PITCHER and Rules 3.06, 8.03.

relieve, v. To come in as a relief pitcher.

reserve clause. A clause in a professional baseball contract which binds a player to a certain team or to some other team to which it may elect to trade or sell him. The player is not a free agent. The reserve clause has been the cause of much legal controversy.

resin bag. A bag of resin placed in back of the pitcher's plate. The pitcher may apply it to his hands, to dry them, but not to the ball.

retire, v. To put out. See OUT and PUTOUT.

retouch, n. The act of a runner in returning to a base as legally required.

rhubarb, (s) n. An altercation or violent dispute.

right field. 1. The outfield territory beyond first base, within the right field foul line (continuation of the first base foul line) and extending to that beyond second base which is covered by the center fielder. 2. The name of the position occupied by the player who covers right field. Abbreviation: rf.

right fielder. An outfielder who is assigned to cover the right field territory.

Rochester Red Wings. The Rochester team of the International League (AAA). A "Northern" team.

rock, (s) n. A stupid or "bone-head" play.

rock, v. To shift balance (by the pitcher) preliminary to pitching. The pitcher often rocks back, then forward.

roller, n. A ground ball.

rookie, (s) n. A new or relatively inexperienced player, such as a first-year man in a big league.

rotation, n. See ROUNDERS.

rounders, n. A term often applied to an old English bat-and-ball game from which baseball is believed, by some, to have at least partially derived. Its modern usage, however, is applied more to the informal type of baseball played more on an individual basis rather than a team vs. team. It also goes by such names as "rotation," "work-up," "scrub," "one old cat," "two old cat," "three old cat." Often the players are small boys, and the game is played when there are not enough players available to form teams. With the exception of "one old cat" (which see) two or three players bat, the rest take the field. Baseball rules apply, but when a batter is put out he immediately takes the field, and the other players move up one position nearer to a batting turn. Usual rotation: retired batter goes to right field: rf. goes to cf.; cf. to lf.; lf. to ss.; ss. to 3b.; 3b. to 2b.; 2b. to 1b., 1b. to p.; p. to c., and the catcher becomes one of the batters. If a fielder catches the ball on the fly, he usually changes places with the retired batter. A force situation at home plate arises when all eligible batters save the actual batter are on base. Otherwise if the bases remained occupied by both, or all three batting players, there would be nobody to bat. The objective is to stay at bat as long as possible and score the most runs during the game (which is often terminated only by darkness or maternal edict when youngsters are playing). Many great players have learned their skills and the basic rules of baseball from rounders. The choice of allowing two or three players to be at bat depends on the number of players available. Should nine fielders be available, there would, as a rule, be three batters (a total of twelve in the game). With over that number a straight team vs. team game would be more likely. With less than a total of twelve, regular rounders—all four bases in use—might be played with two batters, but this is unlikely, because the first of the two batters would have to complete the entire circuit while the second batter was batting. More probable: a game with less bases (only two or one besides home plate) in which case the game is "two old cat" or "one old cat." Rounders with three bases (besides home base) and three batters is the same as "three old cat." The basic principle is: the fewer players available, the fewer batting at once and the fewer bases.

round-house, n. A sweeping but obvious curve—easily hit by experienced batters.

round trip, (s). A home run. Or "round-tripper."

route, (s) n. The entire game. A pitcher going a full nine innings goes the "route."

Royals. The Montreal team of the International League (AAA). A "Northern" team.

rubber, n. 1. A term most often applied to the pitcher's plate, sometimes to home plate. 2. The deciding contest. Example: If each team has won 3 games in a series, the 7th game is the rubber game.

run, n. The game's only scoring unit, achieved when a player legally and safely reaches and touches home plate after touching the other three bases, before three men have been put out. But if he reaches home on or during a play in which the third man is forced out or put out before reaching first base, a run does not count. The same applies if a third out is made by a preceding runner failing to touch a base. Runs may be scored by the awarding of automatic extra bases for ground rules or rule violations, but in all cases the player must touch all bases. The run has a value of 1. See Rules 2.57, 4.09.

run, v. 1. To act as base-runner. A player "runs" the bases. 2. To act as manager or captain—"running" the team.

run-and-hit. A play somewhat similar to the hit-and-run (which see) except that, although the base-runner runs, the batter is not compelled to attempt to hit.

run down. To catch a base-runner between bases and put him out by tagging. Often this requires the ball to be thrown back and forth a number of times between two or more fielders, since the runner dodges back and forth. See Rules 2.58, 7.06(b).

run-down, n. That done when fielders run a base-runner down or attempt to do so.

runner, n. A base-runner (which see).

run out. To run at maximum speed toward first base after making a fair hit. In some cases, when it appears that the batter will inevitably be retired, he fails to do so, in which case he may fail to profit by an unexpected error. Batters are accordingly urged to run out their hits.

runs batted in. An accomplishment credited to batters in the scoring and in season records. A batter is so credited for each run that scores when he makes a base hit, is retired by an infield or outfield putout, and when a run is forced in because he becomes a base-runner—as in the event of a base on balls or the batter hit by a pitched ball. Example: A batter hitting a home run with the bases full gets credit for 4 runs batted in (his own included). If the batter is retired at first base but a runner scores, he gets credit for 1 run batted in. Ordinarily he receives no credit in the event of an error, but should the error be made on a play on which the runner would ordinarily score, he receives such credit. No runs batted in are credited if the batter hits into a force double play or one in which the first baseman picks up a fair hit ball, touches first base and then throws to second, retiring the runner (by a tag) who had been on first. Abbreviation: RBI. See Rule 10.03 (i & j).

rush seat, (s). An unreserved seat. Often a bleacher one.

S

sack, (s) n. A base, except home base.

sacker, (s) n. A baseman. "First-sacker," "second-sacker," "third-sacker."

Sacramento Senators. The Sacramento team of the Pacific Coast League (AAA). A "Southern" team.

sacrifice, n. A sacrifice hit (which see).

sacrifice, v. To make a sacrifice hit (which see).

sacrifice fly. An outfield fly caught by a fielder, after which the runner scores after tagging up. Not an official term, but sometimes used in conversation. It is not credited to the batter as a sacrifice hit, but he does get credit for a run batted in on a putout. Rule 10.03 (i).

sacrifice hit. An achievement credited to a batter who, with none or one out, advances one or more runners by a bunt which results in the batter being put out at first, or would so result if handled without error. If there are two or more runners on base, and any is put out, it is not credited. Abbreviation SH. The batter is not charged with a time at bat. See Rule 10.06.

safe, adj. A term most easily defined as the opposite of out (which see). A player is safe when he reaches a base without being put out. This may be due to a base hit, an opponent's error or lapse of judgment, or an award. He may reach a base due to a sacrifice of a teammate, or steal a base. He is likewise safe if he returns to a base without being put out. See PUTOUT, BASE HIT, ERROR, SACRIFICE HIT, STOLEN BASE, FIELDER'S CHOICE.

safety, (s) n. A base hit.

Saints. The St. Paul team of the American Association (AAA). A "Western" team.

San Diego Padres. The San Diego team of the Pacific Coast League (AAA). A "Southern" team.

sandlot, (s) adj. Pertaining to games played informally in any area which may be made to serve, such as a vacant lot, a pasture, cramped park, yard, etc. Such a player is a "sandlotter." Since most boys start under such conditions, a great many big-leaguers were once sandlotters.

San Francisco Seals. The San Francisco team of the Pacific Coast League (AAA). A "Northern" team.

scalped field. A baseball field having no turf.

scatter-armed, (s) adj. Prone to make wild throws, the term usually applied to a fielder rather than a pitcher.

schedule, n. The list of contests arranged for a team or teams during a given season, specifying the dates, locations and whether or not night games are indicated. The length of the schedule depends on the size of the league and, sometimes on climate. The major league teams play a 154-game schedule, each team playing 22 contests against each of the other seven teams in the league; 11 of these are at home, 11 away, which means that, over a season a team plays 77 games at home, 77 on the road. Each team plays a series of consecutive games against each other team, the series consisting usually of 3 or 2 games (occasionally 4), and it normally plays 8 such series to make up its 22-game quota, 4 of these at home, 4 in the other team's park. For scheduling purposes clubs are classified "Eastern" or "Western," or "Northern" or "Southern" in certain other leagues. See "Eastern" team, etc. An Eastern team takes four Western trips, consecutively playing series against the four Western teams on each trip. It also has four home stands where it meets these clubs in the same fashion. In the intervening time, the Eastern team plays the other three Eastern teams, games equally divided between the home grounds and on the road. Most other leagues use a comparable system.

score, n. The tally, dictated by the number of runs, such as 5 to 3.

score, v. 1. To make a run. 2. To keep the score or scoring records.

scoreboard, n. A large signboard for the convenience of spectators. A first-class one shows the number of outs, strikes, balls, players' positions and numbers, the number of the man at bat, the run score and may also show the scores of other league games in progress.

	4 Wakefield, o.f.	10 Rolfe, mgr.	21 Kell, i.f.	33 Lyons, coach
	5 Vico, i.f.	12 Houtteman, p.	24 Stuart, p.	34 Gray, p.
	6 Mullin, o.f.	18 Overmire, p.	25 Riebe, catcher	36 Kretlow, p.
	8 Berry, i.f.	19 Grissom, p.	28 Bartell, coach	

DETROIT	1	2	3	4	5	6	7	8	9	10		AB	R	H	PO	A	E
15 Campbell first base																	
7 Lake third base																	
20 Wertz right field																	
14 Evers left field																	
3 Groth center field																	
17 Kolloway second base																	
2 Lipon shortstop																	
9 Swift																	
1 Robinson, catcher																	
29 Hutchinson																	
16 Newhouser																	
11 Trout																	
22 Trucks pitcher																	

NUMBER PLAYERS AS FOLLOWS

Pitcher	1	Second Baseman	4	Left Fielder	7
Catcher	2	Third Baseman	5	Center Fielder	8
First Baseman	3	Shortstop	6	Right Fielder	9

SYMBOLS FOR PLAYS

Single	—	Reached base on error	E	Stolen Base	S	Struck Out	K
Double	=	Fielder's Choice	FC	Sacrifice Hit	SH	Base on Balls	BB
Triple	≡	Hit by Pitcher	HP	Passed Ball	PB	Force Out	FO
Home Run		Wild Pitch	WP	Balk	BK		

The lower lefthand corner of the scoring block should be considered as home plate. Progress is counter-clockwise with progress to first base indicated in lower righthand corner, to second in upper righthand corner, to third in upper lefthand corner and to home in lower left. In example to left, batter reached first on an error by the second baseman, stole second, went to third on a wild pitch and scored on a passed ball. It is convenient to circle all runs as shown so that scoring plays may be seen at a glance.

—Courtesy of Harry M. Stevens, Inc. and the Detroit American League Baseball Club

scorecard, n. A card on which score is kept. Usual type is shown above.

scorekeeper, n. A term which, strictly applied, would refer only to the umpire, since he conducts the game and keeps the score.

scorer, n. A term usually applied to a spectator, usually a newspaper reporter, who is designated as "official" scorer. This does *not* mean that he is officially entrusted with the run score, since that is the umpire's province. The "official" scorer evaluates the *quality* of play which is incorporated in the records. He rules—purely for these records—on errors, base hits, times at bat, sacrifice hits, assists, passed balls, wild pitches, runs batted in, stolen bases, earned runs, who is the winning or losing pitcher. See Rules 10.01-10.18 inclusive.

scoring, n. See SCORER.

scout, n. One who engages in scouting (which see).

scout, v. To engage in scouting (which see).

scouting, n. 1. The practice of watching players in minor leagues, colleges, schools, etc., in order to estimate their potential worth as a member of the scout's team. 2. The practice of watching future opponents in action in order to discover their strengths and weaknesses.

scratch hit. A ball not solidly hit, but which results in a base hit. Hence often a lucky or "fluke" hit.

screen, n. A screenwork barrier in front of a grandstand, to protect spectators.

screwball, (s) n. A pitched ball that curves toward a right-handed batter when delivered by a right-handed pitcher, hence an incurve. More rare than the outcurve.

scrub, n. 1. A term often applied to rounders (which see). 2. A substitute or member of a second team.

seagull, (s) n. A scratch hit, in which the bat is broken.

Seals. The San Francisco team of the Pacific Coast League (AAA). A "Northern" team.

Seattle Indians. The Seattle team of the Pacific Coast League (AAA). A "Northern" team.

second, n. Short for second base.

second base. 1. The base to which the base-runner goes after reaching first base, a 15"-square bag, located diagonally left from first base on an imaginary line running through first base at right angles to the right field foul line. The base is centered directly over this line's intersection with another imaginary line from third base at right angles to the left field foul line. The distance from both first and third bases is 90'. Second base is the opposite corner of the diamond (actually a square) from home plate, and is 127' 3⅜" therefrom. See diagram at the beginning of the rules. 2. The position designation of the fielder who normally stands on the first base side of second base. Abbreviation: 2b. He is one of the two players assigned to cover this base, the other being the shortstop (which see).

second baseman. The fielder who habitually covers second base and territory to the first base side of it. He is therefore an infielder.

second division. The half of a league that contains the teams with lowest standing. It denotes the last 4 teams in an 8-team league.

semi-pro, (s). Short for semi-professional.

semi-professional, n. A player who receives money for playing, but who has other employment, often of a more important nature. There are many semi-professional teams throughout the country. A number of these compete for a national championship under the auspices of the National Baseball Congress. Their better players sometimes advance to regular professional minor and major leagues.

series, n. A succession of contests between two teams. These may be regular games on the schedule or play-offs of one type or another. See SCHEDULE, PLAY-OFF, SHAUGHNESSY PLAY-OFFS, WORLD SERIES.

Senators. The Washington team of the American League (major). An "Eastern" team. Also the Sacramento team of the Pacific Coast League (AAA). A "Southern" team.

set position. One of the two legal pitching positions, the pitcher facing the batter with his pivot foot legally on the pitcher's plate, the other foot in front of it, holding the ball in both hands in front of his body and coming to a complete stop of at least one second. See Rule 8.01(b).

shackle, (s) v. To pitch effectively. The batters, unable to hit, are "shackled."

shake off, (s). To refuse to deliver the type of pitch signaled for by the catcher. So-called because the pitcher shakes his head.

Shaughnessy Play-offs. A play-off series in the International League and American Association (both AAA). In each league the teams finishing first and third in the regular schedule play each other a four-out-of-seven-game series. The same is done by the second and fourth-place teams. The winners of these then play another series, thereby deciding the winner in each league. These winners then play a final interleague series, often called the Little World Series. Similar series, involving the four top teams, are played in many other leagues.

shell, (s) v. To bat so hard the pitcher must be taken out. He is "shelled off the mound."

Shibe Park. Home grounds of the Philadelphia Athletics and Philadelphia Phillies. Distance from home plate to right field: 331'; center field: 468'; left field: 334'.

shine ball, (s). A ball which is unnaturally smooth because the pitcher has rubbed it on his glove, person, or clothing, all of which are illegal. This causes the ball to curve to a marked degree. See Rule 8.02.

shoe, n. The footgear worn. The baseball shoe is a low leather one, with spikes on the ball and heel of the sole. See SPIKE.

shoestring catch, (s). A catch made just before the ball hits the ground.

short, n. A short term for shortstop.

short, adv. Relatively near the plate, as where a third baseman plays short (in on the grass) to anticipate a bunt.

shortfield, n. The area between second and third base usually covered by the shortstop.

shortstop, n. An infield position normally to the left (third base) side of second base. The shortstop is one of the two infielders assigned to cover second base, the other one being the second baseman who normally covers territory on the first base side. Abbreviation: ss.

shut out. To prevent the opponents from scoring.

shutout, n. A game in which the losers fail to score.

sidearm, adj. Thrown with the arm at the side of the body, not overhand or underhand. Such a pitching delivery is sometimes termed "crossfire."

sign, n. A signal.

signal, n. A sign, gesture, utterance, etc., intended to guide a player or players. The catcher signals for the type of pitching delivery. Signals are often given by coaches or the manager. Some dictate where fielders should play, what base-runners should do, whether batters should hit or take, or where they should attempt to hit.

signal, v. To make a signal.

simulated play-by-play. A broadcast, after the game is over, which attempts to ape a regular play-by-play broadcast, giving the high spots of the game as though it were actually taking place. Nothing in the Constitution forbids it.

single, n. A base hit on which first base, but no further one, is reached.

single, v. To make a single.

sinker, n. A pitched ball that drops.

skin diamond. A diamond devoid of grass.

slab, (s) n. The pitcher's plate. A pitcher is a "slab artist."

slant, (s) n. A curved pitch.

slice, v. To swing late at the ball when batting. When a right-handed batter "slices" the ball he hits it in the direction of first base and right field, and one who does so consistently is a "slice hitter." Third base and left field for a left-handed batter. The opposite of pulling.

slide, n. That done when a player slides.

slide, v. To slide along the ground toward a base in order to avoid being tagged or to avoid overrunning the base. To over-slide is to slide accidentally beyond the base. Sliding is usually feet-first, but a few players slide head-first. See HOOK SLIDE.

slider, (s) n. A curve ball.

sliding pad. A heavy pad, worn under the pants, to prevent bruises and abrasions from sliding.

slow ball. A pitched ball, delivered with the same motion as a fast ball, but which has less speed, intended to deceive the batter into swinging too soon.

slug, v. To bat hard.

slugfest, (s) n. A game marked by heavy hitting.

slugger, n. A heavy hitter; one who hits long balls.

slugging percentage. A batter's effectiveness in making extra-base hits, determined by dividing his times at bat into his total bases. Example: At bat: 504; total bases: 388; the slugging percentage is .756. See TOTAL BASES.

slump, n. A losing streak or a loss of effectiveness, such as a batting slump.

snap, n. A quick short throw with a snapping wrist motion.

South Atlantic League. One of the four minor leagues in the A classification, the other three being the Central, Eastern and Western

Leagues. There are eight teams: Augusta, Ga.; Charleston, S.C.; Columbia, S.C.; Columbus, Ga.; Greenville, S.C.; Jacksonville, Fla.; Macon, Ga.; Savannah, Ga.

Southern Association. One of the two minor leagues in the AA classification, the other being the Texas League. There are eight teams: the Atlanta Crackers, Birmingham Barons, Chattanooga Lookouts, Knoxville Smokies, Little Rock Travelers, Memphis Chickasaws (or "Chicks"), Nashville Volunteers and New Orleans Pelicans.

Southern team. A team classified as "Southern" in certain leagues for scheduling purposes, such as the Pacific Coast and International Leagues. In the Pacific Coast League the four Southern teams are the Hollywood Stars, Los Angeles Angels, Sacramento Senators, and San Diego Padres. International League: Baltimore Orioles, Jersey City Little Giants, Springfield Cubs and Syracuse Chiefs.

southpaw, (s) n. A player who throws left-handed, notably a pitcher.

Sox, (s). A nickname for the Boston Red Sox and the Chicago White Sox, depending on the context.

spike, n. A metal projection on the bottom of the shoe for better traction. It is part of a triangular plate, and there is one plate on the ball of the shoe, one on the heel, the latter plate smaller. Each plate has three spikes, and these spikes are sharpened thin flanges, roughly ½-inch square,

i.e., not small sharp awl-like points as worn on track shoes.

spike, v. To cut a player with one' spikes, notably in sliding to base, should the baseman get ir the way.

spitball, (s) n. A ball on which the pitcher has spit or is moist be cause he has spit on his glove Likewise the delivery of such ball. It can be made to break more sharply when moistened ir this manner but has long since been ruled illegal. See Rule 8.02(a).

spitter, (s) n. A spitball (which see)

split, v. To win and lose an equal number of games, as in a series o double-header.

Sportsman's Park. Home grounds o the St. Louis Browns and St Louis Cardinals. Distance from home plate to right field: 310′ center field: 425′; left field: 351′

Springfield Cubs. The Springfiel team of the International Leagu (AAA). A "Southern" team.

square stance. A batting stanc where the feet are parallel and i line with the flight of the pitch Also called parallel stance. Se also CLOSED STANCE, OPE STANCE.

squeeze, n. A play in which a batte attempts to score the runner o third (sometimes second) b bunting. The runner sprints fo the plate with the pitch and de pends on the batter to bunt i into fair territory so that a fielde will not have time to relay it t the plate in time to prevent th run. Also called squeeze play. Se Rule 10.06(a).

squeeze, v. To make a squeeze.

squeeze play. See SQUEEZE, n.

stance, n. The position of the feet, notably in batting. See CLOSED STANCE, OPEN STANCE, SQUARE STANCE.

stand, n. An edifice for seating the spectators. Often called stands.

standing, n. The position of a team in a league, or of a player in individual averages.

This final standing illustrates the major league schedule (see SCHEDULE) where each of the eight

FINAL STANDING OF CLUBS

	New York.	Boston.	Cleveland.	Detroit.	Philadel.	Chicago.	St. Louis.	Wash'gtn.	Won.	Lost.	Perc'tage.	Games Behind.
N.Y.....	—	13	12	11	14	15	17	15	97	57	.630	—
ost.......	9	—	8	15	14	17	15	18	96	58	.623	1
lev.......	10	14	—	13	9	15	15	13	89	65	.578	8
et.......	11	7	9	—	14	14	14	18	87	67	.565	10
hil.......	8	8	13	8	—	16	12	16	81	73	.526	16
hic.......	7	5	7	8	6	—	15	15	63	91	.409	34
.L.......	5	7	7	8	10	7	—	9	53	101	.344	44
sh.......	7	4	9	4	6	7	13	—	50	104	.325	47
ost.....	57	58	65	67	73	91	101	104	—	—	—	—

—Courtesy of the New York Times.

clubs plays a 154-game schedule—22 against each of the seven other clubs. The summaries under the Won and Lost columns show that New York won a total of 97 games and lost 57, for a percentage, carried out to three decimal places, of .630. Boston finished 1 game behind, as indicated in the Games Behind column. It would have had to win 1 more game—therefore lose 1 less—to tie. The cross-listing of numbers indicates how each team fared against every other team during the season. New York, for instance, defeated Boston 13 times—as shown by the 13 opposite New York and under Boston—and lost to Boston 9

times, as shown by the 9 opposite Boston and under New York.

stanza, (s) n. An inning.

star, n. An excellent or pre-eminent player. See ALL-STAR.

star, v. To play a pre-eminent or brilliant part in a game.

Stars. The Hollywood team of the Pacific Coast League (AAA). A "Southern" team.

start, v. To be in the line-up at the start of the game. See next term.

starting pitcher. The pitcher nominated to start the game and so announced by the umpire. He must pitch until the first batter has either been put out or reached first base unless, in the umpire's judgment, he suffers a disability which incapacitates him. See Rule 3.07.

steal, n. A stolen base (which see).

steal, v. To achieve a stolen base. See STOLEN BASE.

step in the bucket, (s). To step away from the home plate with the front foot when batting. Often considered poor form, but some effective batters do so.

stick, (s) n. A bat.

stickwork, (s) n. Batting. A good batter exhibits good "stickwork."

St. Louis Browns. A major league team, being a "Western" one in the American League. Home grounds: Sportsman's Park.

St. Louis Cardinals. A major league team, being a "Western" one in the National League. Home grounds: Sportsman's Park.

St. Paul Saints. The St. Paul team of the American Association (AAA). A "Western" team.

stolen base. An achievement credited to a base-runner when he advances a base unaided by a base hit, forceout, balk, hit batter, passed ball, wild pitch, balk, putout or error. It is not credited if he is then retired due to an overslide; when any part of an attempted double or triple steal fails; when the opposing side because of indifference (such as with a large lead) makes no effort to prevent it. However, if a catcher fails to throw to second, fearing a runner may score from third, it is credited. Likewise credited if the catcher fails to throw because the runner has advanced so far that such a throw would be risky or futile. A runner caught in a run-down, off base, is credited with a stolen base if he advances. A wild pitch, passed ball or error *after* the runner starts to steal does not deprive him of credit. Most common stolen base: runner on first base starts for second when the pitcher pitches, and reaches second before the catcher can throw the ball there. Abbreviation: SB. See Rule 10.11.

straight away. Pertaining to orthodox symmetrical positions by fielders rather than shifting to the right or left to anticipate where the batter will hit. A center fielder, for instance, plays straight away when he is on a direct line with second base and home plate.

stranded, (s) adj. Left on base.

stretch, n. 1. The action of the pitcher when he raises both arms, with hands together, over his head before delivering the ball. 2. That done by spectators when they rise from their seats to stretch themselves. The "seventh inning stretch" is a traditional feature of baseball.

stretch, v. 1. To make a stretch in either of the meanings in the preceding term. 2. To make an extra base on a hit by fast bold running. A batter "stretches" a single into a two base hit.

strike, n. A legal pitch when so called by the umpire, which: is struck at by the batter and is missed; enters the strike zone in flight and is not struck at; is fouled by the batter when he has less than two strikes; is bunted foul; hits the batter's person or clothing as he strikes at it; becomes a foul tip. See Rule 2.6 and STRIKEOUT.

strike, v. To swing at and miss the ball, resulting in a strike called.

strikeout, n. A term usually applied to the retirement of the batter due to his being charged with 3 strikes. He is out if the catcher holds the third strike, whether called or swung at. An uncaught foul ball on the third strike does not cause a strikeout; there is no additional count. However, *any* foul bunt on the third strike causes a strikeout. If the catcher drops the ball on a legitimate third strike, the batter is not automatically out if first base is unoccupied. He can attempt to gain first base and must be put out by a force at first or tagging. When there are two out he may attempt this even when first base is occupied. In the usual strikeout the catcher gets credit for the put-out, the pitcher for a strikeout. Should the catcher drop the third strike, and then retire the batter by throwing to first base, the first baseman is credited with a put-out. Even should the batter safely reach first, the pitcher gets credit for a strikeout *unless* he made a wild pitch. See Rule 6.05 (b, c, d, f & h).

strike out, v. To be retired by a strikeout. Practically, as far as batting averages go, the batter strikes out even if *not* retired—as when he reaches first base because of a dropped third strike. He is charged for a time at bat, but not credited with a hit. See STRIKEOUT, n.

strike zone. That space over home plate which is between the batter's armpits and the top of his knees when he assumes his natural stance. Rule 2.63.

stuff, (s) n. What the pitcher puts on the ball—speed, control, curves. A good pitcher has lots of "stuff."

substitute, n. A player not in the original line-up. There is no limit on the number of substitutions except that decreed by the permissible number of active players on a squad. See PINCH HITTER, PINCH RUNNER, RELIEF PITCHER, and Rules 3.03, 3.04, 3.05, 3.06, 3.08, 3.09, 3.10, 3.17.

substitution, n. The entrance of a substitute into a contest. If a player bats for a certain player, he must occupy the place in the batting order held by the player who left the game. See SUBSTITUTE, including cross-references.

sun field. A part of the field where the sun shines directly in a fielder's eyes, notably an outfielder, sometimes necessitating the use of sunglasses.

sunglasses, n. Dark-tinted glasses for protection against sun glare, often used by outfielders. A modern type has a spring which lowers the glass when the fielder desires it.

suspension, n. 1. Temporary cessation of play, due to the ball becoming dead, weather, injuries or other causes. See DEAD BALL; Rules 3.13 and 4.12. 2. Being ruled ineligible to play for a stipulated time, as for flagrant violation of the rules, notably refusal to obey the umpire and tampering with the ball. See Rules 3.02, 4.13 (c), 8.02(a & c).

swing, n. The action of the batter in swinging at the ball.

swing, v. To hit at the ball with the bat. A batter is not considered as swinging if, in the umpire's judgment, he halts the swing before he makes a bona fide effort to meet the ball. See BREAK, v., 3.

swinging bunt. A mis-hit ball, swung at, which has the short slow roll of a bunt. It is not legally a bunt in the rules of the game nor in the scoring rules. See BUNT, n.

switch hitter, (s). A batter who bats either right-handed or left-handed at will, usually depending upon the opposing pitcher.

Syracuse Chiefs. The Syracuse team of the International League AAA. A "Southern" team.

T

tag, n. The action of a fielder in touching a base with his body while holding the ball securely and firmly in his hand or glove; or touching a runner with the ball, or with his glove holding the ball, while holding the ball securely or firmly in his hand or glove. If, when the ball is in play, a runner is so tagged when not in contact with a base, he is out. The ball, however, must be held after tagging, not immediately dropped. It may not even be juggled after tagging, even though the fielder retains possession and does not permit it to drop to the ground. See Rules 2.64, 7.08(c).

tag, v. 1. To touch the base-runner with the ball (by a fielder). 2. Slang for batting the ball hard. The batter "tags" one for a triple.

tag up. To touch a base with the intention of advancing after a batted fly ball is caught. A runner must be in such contact with the base he occupies when or after the ball is caught. If he advances before that instant, he is in danger of being doubled up—put out if the ball is returned to the base before he gets back to it. On a fly of reasonably long depth in the outfield, a runner can score from third base by tagging up—or may advance from first or second to second and third respectively if the ball is a very long one. See Rules 7.08(d), 7.10(a).

tailender, (s) n. A team in last place.

take, (s) v. To let a pitched ball go by (on the part of the batter). If he fails to swing or bunt at it, he

"takes," usually on an order from the manager or coacher.

team, n. The nine players who must be in the game. They are pitcher, catcher, first baseman, second baseman, shortstop, third baseman, left fielder, center fielder, right fielder. Substitutions are permissible, but a team may not play short-handed.

Texas League. One of the two minor leagues in the AA classification, the other being the Southern Association. There are eight teams: the Beaumont Exporters, Dallas Steers, Fort Worth Cats, Galveston Buccaneers, Houston Buffalos, Oklahoma City Indians, San Antonio Missions and Tulsa Oilers.

Texas Leaguer, (s). A batted ball which loops over the infielders' heads but is not driven far enough to be caught on the fly by an outfielder, hence good for a base hit. Also called "blooper."

third, n. Short for third base.

third base. 1. The base to which the base-runner goes after reaching second base. It is a 15″-square bag diagonally to the left from home plate along the left field foul line, fixed exactly within the angle at the intersection of the line from home plate with a line from second base. Its outside edge coincides exactly with the outside edge of the foul line. Distance from rear apex of home plate to the farthest edge of third base: 90′. See BASE and diagram at the beginning of the rules. 2. The position designation of the player who habitually covers third base. Abbreviation: 3b.

third baseman. The player who habitually covers third base, therefore an infielder.

three-bagger, (s) n. A three base hit.

three base hit. A base hit which enables the player making it to reach third base safely without benefit of an error. Abbreviation: 3B.

three hundred hitter. A player whose batting average (which see) is .300 or better (excellent).

three old cat. A game on the same principle as rounders (which see). There are three batters, and all four bases are used.

throw, n. The act of throwing—applied in the rules to a fielder's throw rather than that by the pitcher. See Rule 2.65.

throw, v. To hurl or propel the ball. Sometimes applied to pitching. Jones is now "throwing." See THROW, n.

thrown out. Put out because of the action of a fielder. See THROW OUT.

throw out, 1. To cause a base-runner to be put out by throwing the ball to a baseman at a base. The most common play is the force play in which the batter (now a base-runner) is thrown out at first base. A runner may be thrown out by a force at other bases or may be tagged—as when a catcher throws out a runner attempting to steal. 2. To throw out a ball from the stands, at the start of the season's first game, by a celebrity such as a mayor, gov-

ernor, or the President. "Throwing out the first ball" is a traditional baseball ceremony. 3. Slang for to remove from the game (by the umpire for misconduct).

thumb out, (s). To remove from the game, so-called because the umpire sometimes gestures toward an exit with his thumb. The ejected player "gets the thumb."

tie, n. A regulation game which ends in an equal score, having been terminated by inclement weather, darkness or any other cause. Officially a "regulation drawn game." The "regulation game" proviso is important. See REGULATION GAME. Five or more equal innings must have been played, or the team last at bat must, before the completion of its fifth inning, equal the score made by the opposing team in five complete innings. Should the game be terminated with an equal score for both teams in the fourth inning, for instance, it is *not* a tie game, but simply "no game." See Rule 4.11.

tie, v. To play a tie game.

Tigers. The Detroit team of the American League (major). A "Western" team.

time, n. A term commonly used in baseball to denote suspension of play. The umpire calls "Time" for a legal interruption, as for bad weather, an injury, a batter's request to step out of the batter's box. Time is out until the umpire calls "Play!" See Rules 3.12(d), 3.14, 5.07, 5.10.

tip, n. See FOUL TIP.

toe-plate, n. A metal plate on the toe of the pitcher's pivot foot, serving to protect the toe of this shoe, which constantly digs into the ground.

Toledo Mud Hens (or Mudhens). The Toledo team of the American Association (AAA). An "Eastern" team.

top, n. 1. The first half of an inning, often called "top half." 2. The first part of the batting order—the first four or five batters.

top, v. 1. To bat the ball on the top half, usually resulting in a weak grounder. The ball is not solidly hit. 2. To win.

Toronto Maple Leafs. The Toronto team of the International League (AAA). A "Northern" team.

toss, v. In general, to throw lightly (sometimes underhand), but not always so used in baseball. A fielder "tosses out" (throws out) a runner, and a pitcher is a "tosser."

total bases. The total number of bases a batter reaches solely by virtue of his base hits. A single gives 1 total base; two base hit: 2; three base hit: 3; home run: 4. Should a batter make each of these in a game, he would make 4 hits for 10 total bases. Abbreviation: TB.

total chances. The total number of fielding chances a player has, arrived at by totaling his putouts, assists and errors. Abbreviation: TC.

trap, v. 1. To catch a runner off base. 2. To make a pick-up (which see). Sometimes a fielder deliberately traps a ball he could catch on the fly in order to force a runner who has held his base, fearing a caught fly.

trapper's mitt. A large glove with three compartments, sometimes used by first basemen. The thumb goes in the thumb compartment, all fingers in the third one. The middle one forms the body of the pocket.

Tribe, (s). A term, depending on context, applied to a team with an "Indian" name. Among other it is applied to the Boston Braves, Cleveland, Indianapolis and Seattle Indians.

triple, n. A three base hit.

triple, v. To make a three base hit.

triple play. A play by the defense in which three offensive player are legally put out as a result of continuous play. It is very rare and can occur, of course, only when there are none out. See Rule 2.68.

triple steal. An achievement when each of three base-runners steal a base on the same play.

triple up. To make a triple play.

twilight-night, n. A double-header the first game played late in the afternoon, the second in the evening under lights.

twi-night (s). See TWILIGHT-NIGHT

twin bill, (s). A double-header.

twin killing, (s). A double play.

twirl, (s) v. To pitch.

twirler, (s) n. A pitcher.

two-bagger, (s) n. A two base hit.

two base hit. A base hit which enables the player making it reach second base safely without benefit of error. Abbreviation: 2B.

two old cat. A game on the principle of rounders (which see). There are two batters, and usually only one base besides home plate. A batter making a hit may remain at first base until the other batter hits the ball, whereas in one old cat he would have to run to first base and back to home on his hit. Usually this is played when 6-7 fielders are available. Less would dictate one old cat, more, three old cat. Sometimes two bases besides home are used —first and third bases with second base eliminated.

U

ump (s). Short for umpire.

umpire, n. An official who runs the game and makes decisions. See UMPIRE-IN-CHIEF and FIELD UMPIRE, and Rules 9.01-9.13 inclusive.

umpire, v. To act as an umpire.

umpire-baiter, (s). One who habitually argues with, taunts and otherwise harasses umpires.

umpire-in-chief, n. The chief official who takes a position behind the catcher, and is protected with a chest protector and mask. He has full charge of the game, including responsibility for its proper conduct, and is the sole authority to declare a forfeit. He calls and counts balls and strikes, fair and foul balls (including foul tips), and makes all decisions on the batter. In certain instances he makes base decisions. Should there be but a single umpire, his duties and jurisdiction extend to all points, and he may take any position desirable. One behind the pitcher is common in that case. See Rules 9.06-9.08 inclusive.

underhand, adj. Pertaining to throwing with the hand lower than the elbow. Underhand pitching is rare, but infielders often throw to base underhanded because of insufficient time to straighten up and throw overhanded.

uniform, n. The clothing worn. Major league rules insist on conformity by all players, and call for both home and traveling uniforms, the two to contrast in color and style. The outer garment is usually flannel, more rarely silk, consisting of knickerbocker-type trousers that come somewhat below the knee and a half-sleeve shirt. A full-sleeved jersey is usually worn under the shirt, and sliding pads under the trousers are customary. The stockings are long. Low spiked shoes and a baseball cap complete the uniform. There is lettering or insignia on the shirt and the cap, sometimes on the sleeve, and numbering on the back of the shirt. See Rule 1.15.

up, adj. At bat. The player who is batting is "up."

upstairs, (s). adj. 1. Pertaining to an upper grandstand tier. The batter fouls one "upstairs." 2. Pertaining to a pitched ball which is high.

utility man. A substitute, the term usually applied to one capable of playing several positions, such as

V

vest pocket catch, (s). A catch of a high fly—usually by an infielder —in which the glove is held at,

W

wagon-tongue, (s) n. A bat.

wait out. To make the pitcher throw. The batter may wait out the pitcher, and receive a base on balls.

waiver, n. A system whereby all teams in a league have the chance to bid for a player who is about to be released by a given club, and at a stipulated price, depending on the league. If all clubs waive their right, the player may go to another league.

walk, v. To receive a base on balls.

walk, n. A base on balls.

war club, (s). A bat.

warm up. To practice before a contest—or to do so if one is not in the game—such as a pitcher who warms up in the bullpen.

warm-up, n. That done when one warms up.

warm-up pitch. A practice pitch, at the start of a game or inning or when a pitcher comes in on relief. Eight warm-up pitches not to consume a total time of more than one minute are permitted. See Rule 8.03.

Washington Senators. A major league team, being an "Eastern" one in the American League. Home grounds: Griffith Stadium.

waste ball, (s). A ball deliberately pitched outside the strike zone—

an infielder who can play acceptably at second base, third base or shortstop.

or slightly above, the waist. Also called "breadbasket catch."

usually to entice the batter to swing at it when the pitcher is ahead of the batter.

Western League. One of the four minor leagues in the A classification, the other three being the Central, Eastern and South Atlantic. There were formerly six teams, are now eight, Colorado Springs, Colo., and Wichita, Kansas, having been admitted. The other six are: Denver, Colo.; De Moines, Iowa; Lincoln, Neb.; Omaha, Neb.; Pueblo, Colo.; Sioux City, Iowa.

Western team. A team classified as "Western" for scheduling purposes. In the American League the four Western teams are the Chicago White Sox, Cleveland Indians, Detroit Tigers and St. Louis Browns. National League: Chicago Cubs, Cincinnati Reds, Pittsburgh Pirates and St. Louis Cardinals. American Association: Kansas City Blues, Milwaukee Brewers, Minneapolis Millers and St. Paul Saints.

whiff, (s) v. To strike out swinging. The term is sometimes applied to any swinging strike, but the strike-out meaning is more common.

whip, (s) n. A throwing arm, notably a pitcher's.

whip, v. To make a fast brisk throw. The ball is whipped around the infield.

White Elephants, (s). A nickname for the Philadelphia Athletics.

White Sox. The Chicago team of the American League (major). A "Western" team.

whitewash, (s) v. To hold the opponents scoreless. To shut out.

wide, adj. Far to one side or the other from a base. A wide pitch misses the plate. A wide throw is relatively far from a base—often preventing the would-be receiver from catching it or making a force or tag putout.

wild, adj. Lacking control in throwing, as a wild pitcher or wild-throwing fielder.

wild pitch. A legally-pitched ball so high, wide or low that the catcher cannot or does not stop and control it with ordinary effort, and, as a result, a base-runner advances. Also any pitched ball that strikes the ground before reaching the plate and passes the catcher, allowing a runner or runners to advance. It is therefore the pitcher's fault whereas a passed ball (which see) is the catcher's. However, no error is scored for the pitcher unless the batter reaches first base on it (as he might by swinging at it with two strikes on him) in which case it is not scored as a wild pitch. Abbreviation: WP. See Rules 10.10(b), 10.12.

wild throw. A fielder's wild throw which permits runners to advance. See Rules 7.05 (d, e, f & g), 10.10(c & d).

willow, (s). A bat (although ash is more common).

windup, n. The motion indulged in by the pitcher before delivering the ball to the plate. It is often abbreviated or entirely eliminated with men on base. See PITCHING and STRETCH.

windup position. The pitcher's position when he stands facing the batter, his pivot foot on, or in front of and touching the pitcher's plate, and the other foot free. See Rules 2.69, 8.01(a).

wing, (s) n. A throwing arm, notably a pitcher's.

winning pitcher. The pitcher who is credited with a game won. This includes: one who starts and completes a winning game; one who comes in on relief with his team behind or tied and then completes a winning game; one who comes in on relief with his team behind or tied and then leaves the game with a lead which is not subsequently cancelled or overcome, provided he is judged the most effective of any relief pitchers; one who starts a game and then leaves it with a lead which is not subsequently cancelled or overcome. This starting pitcher, however, must pitch at least five innings, or at least four innings if the game only goes five innings. See Rule 10.16.

wood, (s) n. A bat. See GOOD WOOD.

woodpile, (s) n. A row of bats, such as those sometimes laid parallel in front of a dugout.

work, (s) v. To pitch. Jones "works" in the box.

work up. See ROUNDERS.

World Series. A four-out-of-seven series played, in early October, between the winners of the American and National League (major) championships, consid-

ered the world's championship.

Wrigley Field. Home grounds of the Chicago Cubs. Distance from home plate to right field: 353′; center field: 400′; left field: 355′.

Y

Yankees. The New York team of the American League (major). An "Eastern" team.

Yankee Stadium. Home grounds of

the New York Yankees. Distance from home plate to right field: 296′; center field: 461′; left field: 301′.

OFFICIAL
BASEBALL
RULES

Reprinted by special permission
from OFFICIAL BASEBALL RULES
COMPLETELY REVISED 1950,
Copyrighted 1950, by Albert B. Chandler,
Commissioner of Baseball.

*Recodified, Amended and Adopted
at New York City, December 21, 1949*

Legend: 24-1 means old Rule 24, Sec. 1. N means New wording or material, in black type.

1.00—Objectives of the Game

1.01 BASEBALL is a game between two teams of nine players each with adequate substitutes, coaches and trainers, under direction of a Manager, played in accordance with these rules, under jurisdiction of an umpire or umpires on an enclosed field. **(16, 53, 1, N)**

1.02 THE OBJECT OF EACH TEAM is to win by scoring the more runs. **(N)**

1.03 EACH UMPIRE is the representative of the President of the League, the President of the National Association and the Commissioner of Baseball. **(53, N)**

1.04 THE UMPIRE-IN-CHIEF SHALL ENFORCE THESE RULES. From the moment the umpire-in-chief receives the batting order from the Manager of the home team until termination of the game he shall enforce all of these rules. This shall include control of ground crews, newsmen and photographers, and any other persons whose duties require their presence upon the field. **(53, N)**

1.05 A GAME consists of nine innings, except as otherwise provided, and an inning is that portion of the game during which each team shall play both offensively and defensively. **(N)**

1.06 THE WINNER OF THE GAME shall be that team which shall have scored, in accordance with these rules, the greater number of runs at the conclusion of a regulation game. **(N)**

PLAYING FIELD

1.07 THE PLAYING FIELD SHALL BE laid out in accordance with the measurements indicated on accompanying diagrams. **(N)**

1.08 DIAGRAM. (See Pages 65, 68, and 70)

1.09 THE HOME PLATE and the PITCHER'S PLATE shall be of whitened rubber, anchored in the ground, even with its surface. The home plate, with beveled edges, shall be level with the baselines. The pitcher's plate shall be on a mound 15 inches higher than home plate. The slope from the pitcher's plate to the baselines shall be gradual. **(11, 9-2, N)**

1.10 First, second and third BASES SHALL BE APPROVED BAGS OF WHITE CANVAS, securely anchored in the ground. They shall be 15 inches square and not less than three, nor more than five inches thick, and shall be filled with soft material. **(12, N)**

1.11 ALL PLAYING LINES, including extension of the foul lines on the fences, shall be clearly marked with lime, chalk or other white material. **(13)**

63

1.12 THE HOME CLUB SHALL FURNISH PLAYERS' BENCHES, one each for the home and visiting teams. Such benches shall be not less than twenty-five feet from the base lines. They shall be roofed and shall be enclosed at the back and ends. **(22)**

IN LAYING OUT A BASEBALL FIELD
PROCEED AS FOLLOWS

(SEE DIAGRAMS ON PAGES 65, 68, 70)

With a steel tape, wire or string lay out the base lines and place the home base at desired location, with the back point of the plate set to point due West-South-West if possible so that the least amount of the sun's rays will shine in the eyes of the players.

The home base must be 250 feet from fence or stands along 1st and 3rd base lines; a distance of 320 to 350 feet is preferable.

From home base measure to desired location of second base 127'-3⅜"

From home base measure 90 ft. towards 1st base.

From 2nd base measure 90 ft. towards 1st base.

The intersection of these two 90' measurements establishes 1st base.

Third base is established the same as 1st base.

The distance from home to 2nd base 127'-3⅜"

The distance from 1st base to 3rd base 127'-⅜"

The front of the Pitcher's Plate is 60'-6" from Home Base.

The next batter's circle 37' each side and to the rear of home base.

The Coacher's Box measurements shown on drawing.

The Grandstand or Fence lines 60' from base lines and home base (see drawing).

The backstop line 60' from home base as shown on drawing.

The Grass line dimensions shown on drawing.

The Catcher's Box dimensions shown on drawing.

The 3 foot lines shown on drawing.

All measurements from Home Base taken from point where 1st and 3rd Base lines intersect.

The Bases—First, Second and Third bases must be a white canvas bag 15" square, not less than 3" nor more than 5" in thickness filled with soft material and securely fastened in place by pegs driven into ground, all distance between bases 90' (see drawing marked A). Angle between base lines 90°.

The Batter's Lines or Batter's Box—On either side of Home Base construct a 4' x 6' rectangle batter's box, located in respect to Home Base as shown on drawing B, to be marked with 2" wide lime, chalk or other white material.

The Catcher's Lines—The back of the Catcher's Box is 8' back of Home Base and 8' each side of Home Base line. Lines to be marked with lime, chalk or other white material 2" wide (see drawing marked C).

Home Base—to be of whitened rubber, point of which to be placed at intersection of 1st and 3rd base lines, so fixed in the ground as to be even with ground surface, edges of Home Base to be beveled (see drawing marked D for layout).

The Pitcher's Plate—To be of whitened rubber 24" x 6" located 60'-6" from Home Base, 12" each side of a line from Home Base to Second Base and must be placed 15" above the base lines and Home Base, slope from Pitcher's Plate to base lines and Home Base shall be gradual (see drawing marked E).

The Next Batter's Circles—37 feet on either side of a line extending from 2nd base to Home Base and to the rear of Home Base describes circles 5' in diameter, mark with lime, chalk or other white material (see drawing).

The Foul Lines—Lines 3" wide extending from the point of Home Base along 1st and 3rd base lines a minimum of 250' to stands or fence, preferably 320 to 350 feet, lines to be marked with lime, chalk or other white material.

The Coacher's Lines—Coacher's Boxes located at 1st and 3rd base corners. 20' long and 10' wide, to be located as shown on drawing. To be marked with lime, chalk or other white material.

The Three-Foot Line—Located along 1st base line, beginning 45' from Home Base and extending 3' beyond 1st and 2nd base line. To be marked with 2" wide lime, chalk or other white material (see drawing).

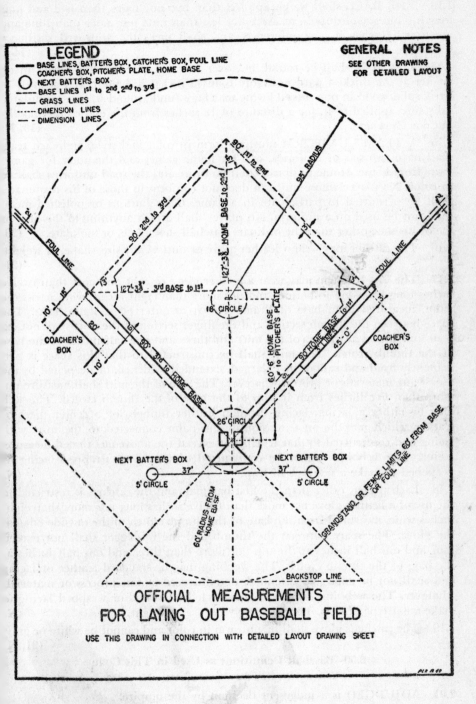

OFFICIAL MEASUREMENTS
FOR LAYING OUT BASEBALL FIELD

USE THIS DRAWING IN CONNECTION WITH DETAILED LAYOUT DRAWING SHEET

1.13 THE BALL shall weigh not less than five nor more than five and one fourth ounces avoirdupois, measure not less than nine nor more than nine and one-fourth inches in circumference, and shall meet the approved resiliency standards.   (14-1

1.14 THE BAT shall be round, not over two and three-fourths inches in di ameter at the thickest part, not more than 42 inches in length, and entirely of hard, solid wood in one piece. Twine may be wound around it, or a granulated substance applied to it, for a distance of 18 inches from the end of the handle but not elsewhere.   (15, N

1.15 A TEAM'S UNIFORM must conform in color and style, and each team shall have two sets of uniforms, one for home games and the other for games away from home. Home uniforms shall be white and the road uniforms shall be in color. No player whose uniform does not conform to those of his teammates shall be permitted to participate in a game. Glass buttons or polished metal shall not be used on a uniform. No player shall attach anything to the heel or toe of his shoe other than the ordinary baseball shoe plate, or toe plate.   (20

1.16 The catcher may wear a leather glove or mitt of any size, shape, or weight   (21

1.17 The first baseman may wear a leather glove or mitt not more than twelve inches long from top to bottom and not more than eight inches wide across the palm, measured from base of thumb crotch to outer edge of the mitt. The space between the thumb section and the finger section of the mitt shall not ex ceed four inches at the top of the mitt and three and one-half inches at the base of the thumb crotch. The mitt shall be constructed so that this space is per manently fixed and cannot be enlarged, extended, widened, or deepened by the use of any materials or process whatever. The web of the mitt shall measure no more than five inches from its top to the base of the thumb crotch. The web may be either a lacing, lacing through leather tunnels, or a center piece of leather which may be an extension of the palm connected to the mitt with lacing and constructed so that it will not exceed the above-mentioned measure ments. The webbing cannot be constructed of wound or wrapped lacing or deepened to make a net type of trap.   (N

1.18 Each player, other than the first baseman and the catcher, is restricted to the use of a leather glove not more than twelve inches long nor more than eight inches wide, measured from the base of the thumb crotch to the outside edge of the glove. The space between the thumb and the forefinger shall not exceed four and one-half inches at the top nor more than three and one-half inches at the base of the thumb crotch. The webbing may be standard leather or lacing and shall not be enlarged, extended, or reinforced by any process or material whatever. The webbing cannot be constructed of wound or wrapped lacing to make a net type of trap. The glove may be of any weight.   (N

1.19 The pitcher's glove shall be uniform in color and cannot be white or gray   (21, N

2.00—Baseball Definitions as Used in This Code
(Numbers following definitions refer to this code.)

2.01 ADJUDGED is a judgment decision by the umpire.

2.02 AN APPEAL is the act of a defensive player in claiming violation of the rules by the offensive team. 7.10.

2.03 APPROVED is the official stipulation with reference to playing equipment.

2.04 A BALK is an illegal act by pitcher or catcher with a runner or runners on base, entitling all runners to advance one base. 8.05.

2.05 A "BALL" is a pitch which does not enter the strike zone in flight and is not struck at by the batter.

2.06 A BASE is one of the four objectives to be touched or occupied by runners on their legal advance to home base and a score.

2.07 A BASE ON BALLS is an award of first base granted to a batter who, during his time at bat, receives four pitches outside the strike zone. 6.07 (a).

2.08 A BATTER is an offensive player who takes his position in the batter's box.

2.09 The BATTER'S BOX is the area within which the batter shall stand during his time at bat.

2.10 The BATTERY is the pitcher and the catcher.

2.11 The BENCH is the seating facilities reserved for players, substitutes and other team members in uniform when they are not actively engaged on the playing field. The bench is sometimes located in an area below the surface of the ground and, when so located, known as the dugout. 3.17; 4.08.

2.12 A BUNT is a legally batted ball not swung at, but intentionally met with the bat and tapped slowly within the infield.

2.13 A CALLED GAME is one in which because of darkness, rain or other legal reason, an umpire-in-chief terminates play.

2.14 A CATCH is the act of a defensive player in receiving, and holding firmly in his hand or glove, a batted or thrown ball. It is not a catch, however, if simultaneously or immediately following his contact with the ball, he collides with a player, or with a wall, or if he falls down, and as a result of such collision or falling, drops the ball. If the player has made the catch and drops the ball while in the act of making a throw following the catch, the ball shall be adjudged to have been caught. In establishing the validity of the catch the player shall hold the ball long enough to prove that he has complete control of the ball and that his release of the ball is voluntary and intentional.

2.15 The CATCHER is a defensive player who takes his position back of the home base.

2.16 The CATCHER'S BOX is that area within which the catcher must stand until the pitcher delivers the ball.

2.17 The COACHER is that team member who occupies the coacher's box at first or third base to direct the base runner or the batter. 4.05.

2.18 A DEAD BALL is a ball out of play because of a legally created temporary suspension of play. 5.09.

2.19 The DEFENSE (or DEFENSIVE) is the team, or any player of the team, in the field.

2.20 A DOUBLE-HEADER is two regularly scheduled or re-scheduled games, played in immediate succession. 4.12.

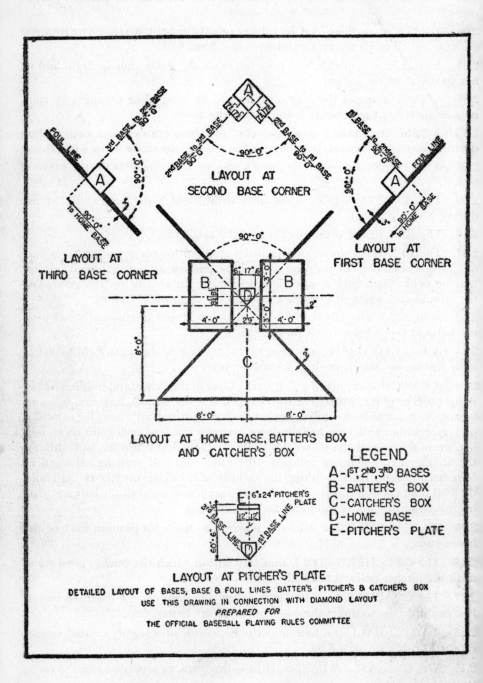

LAYOUT AT SECOND BASE CORNER

LAYOUT AT THIRD BASE CORNER

LAYOUT AT FIRST BASE CORNER

LAYOUT AT HOME BASE, BATTER'S BOX AND CATCHER'S BOX

LEGEND
A - 1ST, 2ND, 3RD BASES
B - BATTER'S BOX
C - CATCHER'S BOX
D - HOME BASE
E - PITCHER'S PLATE

LAYOUT AT PITCHER'S PLATE

DETAILED LAYOUT OF BASES, BASE & FOUL LINES BATTER'S PITCHER'S & CATCHER'S BOX
USE THIS DRAWING IN CONNECTION WITH DIAMOND LAYOUT
PREPARED FOR
THE OFFICIAL BASEBALL PLAYING RULES COMMITTEE

2.21   A DOUBLE PLAY is a play by the defense in which two offensive players are legally put out as a result of continuous play.

2.22   A DUGOUT is the seating facilities reserved for players, substitutes and other team members in uniform when they are not actively engaged on the playing field, and is located in an area below the surface of the ground. The dugout is sometimes located in an area level with the surface of the playing field and, when so located, is known as the bench.

2.23   A FAIR BALL is a legally batted ball that settles on fair ground between home and first base, or between home and third base, or that is on or over fair territory when bounding to the outfield past first base or third base, or that touches first or third base, or that first falls on fair territory on or beyond first base or third base; or that, while on or over fair territory, touches the person of the umpire or player. A fair fly must be judged according to the relative position of the ball and the foul line, including the foul pole, and not as to whether the fielder is on fair or foul territory at the time he touches the ball.

2.24   FAIR TERRITORY is that part of the playing field within, and including the first base and third base lines, from home base to the bottom of the playing field fence and perpendicularly upwards. All foul lines are in fair territory.

2.25   A FIELDER is any defensive player.

2.26   A FLY BALL is a batted ball that goes high in the air in flight.

2.27   A FORCE PLAY is a play in which a runner legally loses his right to occupy a base by reason of the batter becoming a base runner.

2.28   A FORFEITED GAME is a game declared ended by the umpire-in-chief in favor of the offended team by the score of 9 to 0, for violation of the rules. 4.13.

2.29   A FOUL BALL is a legally batted ball that settles on foul territory between home and first base, or between home and third base, or that bounds past first or third base on or over foul territory, or that first falls on foul territory beyond first or third base, or, while on or over foul territory, touches the person of the umpire or a player, or any object foreign to the natural ground. A foul fly shall be judged according to the relative position of the ball and the foul line, including the foul pole, and not as to whether the fielder is on foul or fair territory at the time he touches the ball.

2.30   FOUL TERRITORY is that part of the playing field outside the first and third base lines extended to the fence and perpendicularly upwards.

2.31   A FOUL TIP is a ball batted by the batter that goes sharp and direct from the bat to the catcher's hands and is legally caught. It is not a foul tip unless caught and any foul tip that is caught is a strike, and the ball is in play. It is not a catch if it is a rebound from any part of the catcher's equipment other than the catcher's glove or hand.

2.32   A GROUND BALL is a batted ball that rolls or bounces close to the ground.

2.33   The HOME TEAM is the team on whose grounds the game is played, or if the game is played on neutral grounds, the home team shall be designated by mutual agreement.

2.34   ILLEGAL (or ILLEGALLY) is contrary to these rules.

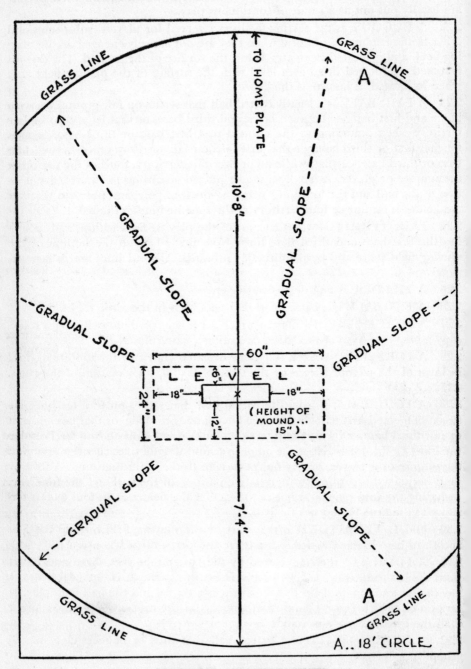

**OFFICIAL MEASUREMENTS
FOR LAYING OUT THE PITCHER'S MOUND**

2.35 An ILLEGAL PITCH is a pitch delivered to the batter when the pitcher is not in pitching position.

2.36 An INFIELDER is a defensive player who occupies a position in the infield.

2.37 **An INFIELD-FLY is an out called by the umpire on the batter**—If, before two are out, while the first and second or first, second and third bases are occupied, he hit a fair fly ball, other than a line drive, that in the judgment of the umpire can reasonably be caught by an infielder. Where a defensive player who normally plays in the outfield places himself in the infield, he shall for the purpose of the Infield-Fly rule be considered an infielder. In such case the umpire shall declare it an INFIELD-FLY. However, the runners may be off their bases or advance at the risk of the ball being caught, the same as on any other fly ball. If a runner is hit by the ball while standing on base, he shall not be called out, but the ball is dead and the batter shall be called out; but if a base runner is hit while off base, both he and the batter shall be called out and the ball is dead. Provided, that, with first and second bases occupied, or first, second and third bases occupied, before two are out, any attempt to bunt which results in a fair fly ball shall not be regarded as an Infield-Fly.

2.38 IN FLIGHT describes a batted, thrown, or pitched ball which has not yet touched the ground or some object other than a fielder.

2.39 IN JEOPARDY is a term indicating that the ball is in play and an offensive player may be put out.

2.40 An INNING is that portion of a game within which the teams alternate on offense and defense and in which there are three putouts for each team.

2.41 LEGAL (or LEGALLY) is in accordance with these rules.

2.42 A LIVE BALL is a ball which is in play.

2.43 OFFENSE is the team, or any player of the team, at bat.

2.44 The OFFICIAL RULES are the rules in this code.

2.45 The OFFICIAL SCORER is an accredited representative of the President of the League. He is an actual official of any championship game whose decisions in scoring the games are final and official.

2.46 An OUT is one of the three required retirements of an offensive team during its time at bat.

2.47 An OUTFIELDER is a defensive player who occupies a position in the outfield which is the area of the playing field most distant from home base.

2.48 OVERSLIDE (or OVERSLIDING) is the act of an offensive player when his slide to a base, other than when advancing from home to first base, is with such momentum that he loses contact with the base, which act places him in jeopardy.

2.49 A PENALTY is the application of these rules following an illegal act.

2.50 The PERSON OF A PLAYER OR UMPIRE is any part of his body, his clothing or his equipment.

2.51 A PITCH is a ball delivered to the batter by the pitcher. 8.01.

2.52 A PITCHER is the defensive player designated to deliver the pitch to the batter. 8.01.

2.53 The pitcher's PIVOT FOOT is that foot which is in contact with the pitcher's plate as he delivers the pitch. 8.01.

2.54 "PLAY" is the umpire's order to start the game or to resume action following any dead ball.

2.55 A REGULATION GAME is nine innings unless shortened or lengthened legally.   4.10.

2.56 A RETOUCH is the act of a runner in returning to a base as legally required.

2.57 A RUN (or SCORE) is the score made by an offensive player who advances from batter to base runner and touches first, second, third and home bases in that order.   4.09.

2.58 A RUN-DOWN is the act of the defense in an attempt to put out an offensive player between bases.   7.06 (b).

2.59 A RUNNER (or BASE RUNNER) is an offensive player who is advancing toward, or touching, or returning to any base.

2.60 "SAFE" is a declaration by the umpire that a runner is entitled to the base for which he was trying.

2.61 SET POSITION is the pitcher's position when he stands facing the batter with his entire pivot foot on, or in front of and in contact with, and not off the end of the pitcher's plate, and his other foot in front of the pitcher's plate, holding the ball in both hands in front of his body and **coming to a complete stop of at least one second.**   8.01 (b).

2.62 A STRIKE is a legal pitch when so called by the umpire, which—
  (a) Is struck at by the batter and is missed;
  (b) Enters the strike zone in flight and is not struck at;
  (c) Is fouled by the batter when he has less than two strikes;
  (d) Is bunted foul;
  (e) Hits the batter's person or clothing as he strikes at it; or
  (f) Becomes a foul tip.

2.63 THE STRIKE ZONE is that space over home plate which is between the batter's armpits and the top of his knees when he assumes his natural stance.

2.64 A TAG is the action of a fielder in touching a base with his body while holding the ball securely and firmly in his hand or glove; or touching a runner with the ball, or with his glove holding the ball, while holding the ball securely or firmly in his hand or glove.

2.65 A THROW is the act of propelling the ball with the hand and arm of the player to a given objective and is to be distinguished, always, from the pitch.

2.66 A TIE GAME is a legal game that ends when the score is even.   4.11.

2.67 "TIME!" is the announcement by an umpire of a legal interruption of play, during which the ball is dead.

2.68 A TRIPLE PLAY is a play by the defense in which three offensive players are legally put out as a result of continuous play.

2.69 WIND-UP POSITION is the pitcher's position when he stands facing the batter, his pivot foot on, or in front of and touching the pitcher's plate, and the other foot free.   8.01 (a).

3.00—Game Preliminaries

3.01 BEFORE THE GAME BEGINS THE UMPIRE SHALL—
  (a) Require strict observance of all rules governing implements of play and equipment of players;

(b) Require all playing lines (heavy lines on the diagram) to be marked with lime, chalk or other white material easily distinguishable from the ground or grass;   (13)

(c) Receive from the home club a supply of regulation baseballs, the number and make to be certified to the home club by the President of the League. Each ball shall be enclosed in a sealed package bearing the signature of the President of the League, and the seal shall not be broken until just prior to game time when the umpire shall open each package to inspect the ball and remove its gloss. The umpire shall be the sole judge of the fitness of balls to be used in the game;   (14-2, 5)

(d) Be assured by the home club that at least one dozen regulation reserve balls are immediately available for use if required;   (14-6)

(e) Have in his possession at least two alternate balls and shall require replenishment of such supply of alternate balls as needed throughout the game. Such alternate balls shall be put in play when—   (14-2)

   1. A ball has been batted out of the playing field or into the spectator area;   (14-2)
   2. A ball has become discolored or unfit for further use;   (14-4)
   3. The pitcher requests such alternate ball, which shall not be delivered to the pitcher until the previously used ball is dead. (14-4, N)

3.02 No player shall INTENTIONALLY DISCOLOR OR DAMAGE THE BALL by rubbing it with soil, rosin, paraffin, licorice, sand-paper, emery-paper or other foreign substance.   (14-4)

PENALTY

The umpire shall demand the ball and remove the offender from the game. In case the umpire cannot locate the offender, and if the pitcher delivers such discolored or damaged ball to the batter, the pitcher shall be removed from the game at once and shall be suspended automatically for ten days.

3.03 During a championship game each team shall have a sufficient number of SUBSTITUTES to meet the requirements of this code.   (17-1)

3.04 A PLAYER, OR PLAYERS, MAY BE SUBSTITUTED during a game at any time the ball is dead. A substituted player shall bat in the replaced player's position in the team's batting order. A player once removed from a game shall not re-enter that game. If a substitute enters the game in place of a Manager, the Manager may thereafter go to the coaching lines at his discretion. When two or more substitute players of the defensive team enter the game at the same time, the Manager, or his designated representative, shall, immediately before they take their position as defensive players, designate to the umpire-in-chief such players' positions in the team's batting order and the umpire-in-chief shall so notify the official scorer. If this information is not immediately given to the umpire-in-chief, he shall have authority to designate the substitutes' places in the batting order.   (17-2, N)

3.05 A player whose name is on his team's batting order MAY NOT BECOME A SUBSTITUTE RUNNER for another member of his team. (17-3, N)

3.06 If a PITCHER IS REPLACED, his substitute shall pitch to the batter then at bat until such batter is retired or reaches first base, or until the inning ends, unless the substitute pitcher sustains an injury which, in the umpire-in-chief's judgment, incapacitates him for further play as a pitcher.   (17-4)

3.07 Formal EXCHANGE OF BATTING ORDERS at home plate, as hereafter stipulated, constitutes an umpire's official announcement of each team's players. Each pitcher thus announced shall pitch to the first batter until the batter is put out or reaches first base, unless he sustains an injury which, in the judgment of the umpire-in-chief, incapacitates him from pitching.   **(17-5, 35)**

3.08 The Manager of a team or his designated representative shall immediately NOTIFY THE UMPIRE-IN-CHIEF of any substitution and shall state to the umpire-in-chief the substitute's place in his batting order.   **(17-6)**

PENALTY

The President of the League shall assess a fine not to exceed $25.00 upon the Manager or his designated representative who fails to notify the umpire of a substitution.   **(N)**

3.09 The UMPIRE-IN-CHIEF, after having been notified, SHALL IMMEDIATELY ANNOUNCE, or cause to be announced, each substitution. **(17-6)**

PENALTY

The President of the League shall assess a fine not to exceed $25.00 upon the umpire for each failure to announce a substitution.   **(N)**

3.10 (a) If, through oversight, NO ANNOUNCEMENT of a SUBSTITUTION is made, the substitute shall be considered as having entered the game when—   **(17-6)**

    (1) If a pitcher, he takes his place on the pitcher's plate;

    (2) If a batter, he takes his place in the batter's box;

    (3) If a fielder, he reaches the position usually occupied by the previous fielder;

    (4) If a runner, he takes the place of the previous runner.

(b) Any play made by, or on, any of the above mentioned unannounced substitutes shall be legal under these rules.   **(17-6)**

3.11 Players in uniform SHALL NOT ADDRESS OR MINGLE with spectators, nor sit in the stands before or during a game. No manager, captain, coacher or player shall address any spectator before or during a game. Players of opposing teams shall not fraternize at any time while in uniform.   **(N)**

PENALTY

The President of the League shall impose fines, for violation of this rule, at his discretion.   **(N)**

3.12 THE SOLE JUDGE OF THE FITNESS OF THE PLAYING FIELD FOR PLAY:—

    (a) THE MANAGER of the home team shall be the sole judge of the fitness of the playing field for the beginning of any game other than the second game of a double-header.   **(26)**

    (b) EXCEPTION: Any league may permanently authorize its President to suspend the application of this rule as to that league during the closing weeks of its championship seasons in order to assure that the championship is decided each year on its merits. When the postponement of, and possible failure to play, a game in the final series of a championship season between any two teams might affect the final standing of any club in the league, the President, on appeal from any league member, may assume the authority granted the Home Team Manager by this rule. **(N)**

(c) THE UMPIRE-IN-CHIEF of the first game shall be the sole judge of the fitness of the playing field for the beginning of the second game of a double-header. **(26)**

(d) THE UMPIRE-IN-CHIEF shall be the sole judge of the fitness of the playing field for the resumption of play after "time" has been called and play suspended during a game. **(26)**

3.13 Between games of a double-header, or whenever a GAME IS SUSPENDED because of the unfitness of the playing field, the umpire-in-chief shall have control of ground keepers and assistants for the purpose of making the playing field fit for play. **(26)**

PENALTY

For violation, the umpire-in-chief may forfeit the game to the visiting team.

3.14 When the umpire SUSPENDS PLAY for legal cause he shall call "TIME." At the umpire's call of "Play," the suspension is lifted and play resumes. Between the call of "Time" and the call of "Play" the ball is dead. **(67-3)**

3.15 The Manager of the home team shall present to the Umpire-in-chief and the opposing Manager or Captain any GROUND RULES he thinks necessary covering the overflow of spectators upon the playing field, batted or thrown balls into such overflow, or any other contingencies. If these rules are acceptable to the opposing Manager they shall be legal. If these rules are unacceptable to the opposing Manager, the Umpire-in-chief shall make and enforce any special ground rules he thinks are made necessary by ground conditions, provided they do not conflict with the official playing rules. He shall cause such special rules to be announced to the spectators. **(65)**

3.16 NO PERSON SHALL BE ALLOWED ON THE PLAYING FIELD during a game except players and coaches in uniform, managers, news photographers authorized by the home team, umpires, designated officers of the law in uniform and watchmen or other employees of the home club. In case of any interference with play by any person herein authorized to be on the playing field, except umpires, the ball is alive and in play unless in the umpire's judgment, the interference is intentional. If the interference is intentional, the ball is dead at the moment of the interference and the umpire shall award the runner one base beyond the base to which he was advancing when the interference occurred. **(68)**

3.17 Players and substitutes of both teams shall confine themselves to their team's bench or dugout unless actually participating in the play or preparing to enter the game, or coaching. No one except players, substitutes, Managers, coaches, trainers and bat boys shall occupy a bench or dugout during a game. **(22)**

PENALTY

For violation the umpire may, after warning, remove the offender from the field. If the offender fails to obey the order in one minute he shall be liable to a fine by the President of the League. **(22-2, N)**

3.18 The home team shall provide POLICE PROTECTION sufficient to preserve order. If a person, or persons, enter the playing field during a game and interfere in any way with the play, the visiting team may refuse to play until the field is cleared. **(68-2)**

PENALTY

If the field is not cleared in a reasonable length of time, which shall in no case be less than fifteen minutes after the visiting team's refusal to play, the umpire may forfeit the game to the visiting team.   **(N)**

3.19 Before the game begins the umpire shall announce or cause to be announced, all special ground rules necessitated by an overflow crowd or any agreement of the opposing managers to stop play at a specified hour.   **(66)**

4.00—Starting and Ending a Game

4.01 Unless the home club shall have given previous notice that the game has been postponed or will be delayed in starting, five minutes before the hour set for the game to begin, the UMPIRE, or UMPIRES, shall enter the playing field and proceed directly to HOME BASE where they shall be met by the managers of the opposing teams, or their representatives.   **(N)**

In sequence—

  (a) First, the home manager must give his batting order to the umpire-in-chief, in duplicate;   **(35)**

  (b) Next, the visiting manager must give his batting order to the umpire-in chief, in duplicate;   **(N)**

  (c) The umpire-in-chief shall retain originals of the respective BATTING ORDERS and hand the duplicates to each opposing manager. Acceptance by the manager of his opponent's batting order constitutes announcement of the batting orders. Thereafter, no substitutions shall be made by either manager, except as provided in these rules.   **(35, N)**

  (d) As soon as the home team's batting order is handed to the umpire-in-chief the umpires are in charge of the playing field and from that moment they shall have sole authority to determine when a game shall be called, suspended or resumed on account of weather or the condition of the playing field.   **(N)**

  (e) GENERAL AND SPECIAL GROUND RULES shall be presented by the home manager and, upon agreement by the visiting manager, become legal. In case of disagreement the umpire-in-chief shall make and enforce such rules as may be necessary, and such rules are legal.   **(65)**

4.02 The players of the HOME TEAM shall take their DEFENSIVE POSITIONS, the first batter of the visiting team shall take his position in the batter's box, the umpire shall call "Play" and the game shall proceed.   **(N)**

4.03 When the ball is put in play at the start of, or during a game, ALL DEFENSIVE PLAYERS other than the catcher must be on FAIR TERRITORY.

  (a) The catcher must stand with both feet within the catcher's box until the ball leaves the pitcher's hand;   **(18)**

  (b) The pitcher, while in the act of delivering the ball to the batter, must take his legal position;   **(18)**

  (c) Except the batter, or a runner attempting to score, no offensive player shall cross the catcher's lines when the ball is in play.   **(18-2, N)**

4.04 THE BATTING ORDER MUST BE FOLLOWED THROUGHOUT THE GAME unless a player is substituted for another. In that case the substitute must take the place of the replaced player in the batting order.   **(35)**

4.05 The offensive team shall be allowed TWO COACHERS ONLY, one near first base and one near third base. Coachers shall—   **(51)**

(a) Be in uniform of their team;

(b) Remain within the coacher's box at all times;

(c) Address players of their own team, only;

(d) Avoid the use of language which will, in any manner, refer to or reflect upon a player of the opposing team, an umpire, or any spectator;

(e) Avoid inciting or trying to incite the spectators to demonstrations by word or sign.

PENALTY

The offender shall be removed from the game and shall leave the playing field.

4.06 No manager, player, substitute, coacher, trainer, or batboy shall at any time, whether from the bench, the coacher's box or on the playing field, or elsewhere—   **(51)**

(a) INCITE, or try to incite, by word or sign a DEMONSTRATION BY SPECTATORS;

(b) Use LANGUAGE which will in any manner refer to, or REFLECT upon opposing players, an umpire, or any spectator;

(c) Call "Time," or employ any other word or phrase while the ball is alive and in play for the obvious purpose of confusing an umpire or an opposing player.   **(N)**

PENALTY

The offender shall be removed from the game and shall leave the playing field.

4.07 When a manager, player, trainer or coacher is REMOVED FROM THE GAME he shall go to the club house. He shall remain in the club house or leave the grounds.   **(60-1)**

4.08 When the occupants of a PLAYER'S BENCH SHOW VIOLENT DIS- APPROVAL of an umpire's decision, the umpire shall first give warning that such disapproval shall cease. If such action continues—   **(60-3)**

PENALTY

The umpire shall order the offenders from the bench to the club house. If he is unable to detect the offender, or offenders, he may clear the bench of all substitute players. The manager or captain of the offending team shall have the privilege of recalling to the playing field only those players needed for substitution in the game.

4.09 One run shall be scored every time a runner, after having legally touched the first three bases, shall legally touch home base before three men are put out; provided, however, that if he reaches home base on or during a play in which the third man is forced out or is put out before reaching first base, his run shall not count; also, if the third out is made by a preceding runner failing to touch a base, the run shall not count.   **(52)**

4.10 IT IS A REGULATION GAME WHEN—

(a) The home team shall have scored more runs in eight innings than the visiting team has scored in nine innings;   **(23-1)**

(b) The home team scores the winning run in the ninth inning before the third man is out. If a batter in the last half of the final inning of a game hits a home run over the fence or into a stand, all runners on base at the time, as well as the batter, shall be entitled to score, but to score legally, all bases must be touched in order by all runners. The final score of such game shall be the total number of runs made by each team;   (23-2)

(c) If the score is even at the end of nine completed innings, play is continued until one team has scored more runs than the other in an equal number of innings; provided, that if the home team scores the winning run before the third man is out in any inning after the ninth, the game shall terminate and be a regulation game;   (23-4)

(d) Terminated by the umpire on account of rain, or darkness, or other cause which makes further play impossible, provided five or more innings have been played, or the home team has scored more runs in four innings, or before the completion of its fifth inning, than the visiting club has scored in five completed innings;   (23-3)

(e) The umpire terminates play after five full innings have been completed, and the score of such game shall be that at the end of the last completed inning. If, however, the home team shall have scored more total runs than the visiting team when the game is terminated while the home team is at bat, the score of such game shall be the total runs scored by each team.   (23-2)

4.11   A REGULATION DRAWN GAME shall be declared by the umpire-in-chief if he terminates play because of rain, darkness, or for any other cause that makes further play impossible—   (23-5)

(a) If, after five or more completed innings, the score is tied;

(b) If, after five or more completed innings, the home team is at bat when play terminates and scores enough runs in an incompleted inning to make its total score equal the visiting team's total score;

(c) If the home team shall score, in its incomplete fifth inning, a run or runs to equal the visiting team's total score in its five complete innings.

4.12   RULES GOVERNING DOUBLE-HEADERS   (N)

(a) Only TWO CHAMPIONSHIP GAMES SHALL BE PLAYED WITHIN A PERIOD OF ONE DAY but if two games are scheduled to be played in one afternoon, the first game shall be the regular game for that day.   (23-7)

(b) By mutual agreement, before the start of the first game of a double-header, upon approval of such agreement by the President of the League, one of the games of such double-header may be designated as a SEVEN INNING GAME and such game shall be a championship game.   (23-8, N)

(c) After the start of the first game of a double-header, that game shall be completed before the second game of the double-header shall begin. (N)

(d) The second game of a double-header shall begin TWENTY MINUTES after completion of the first game, UNLESS a longer interval between games is declared by the umpire-in-chief and announced to the opposing Managers at the conclusion of the first game. The umpire-in-chief of the first game shall be the timekeeper controlling the interval between games.   (24-9, N)

(e) The umpire SHALL START THE SECOND GAME of a double-header, if at all possible, and play shall continue as long as ground conditions, local time restrictions, or weather permit.   (N)

(f) If a NIGHT double-header, or a TWILIGHT-NIGHT DOUBLE-HEADER is scheduled, and if the start of such double-header is delayed for any cause, the umpire shall order playing field lights to be turned on at his discretion so that play may continue without interruption. **(N)**

(g) When a regularly scheduled double-header is delayed in starting by rain or other cause, ANY GAME that is started IS THE FIRST GAME of the double-header. **(N)**

(h) When a RESCHEDULED GAME is part of a double-header the rescheduled game shall be the second game, and the first game shall be the regularly scheduled game for that date. **(N)**

(i) When a portion of a SUSPENDED game is to be completed it shall be played preliminary to the regularly scheduled game for that date. **(N)**

(j) When a LIGHT FAILURE causes suspension of a game and such game is rescheduled for another date, it shall be resumed at the point of interruption of the original game, with the same personnel of the original game, as nearly as possible, and shall be completed preliminary to the regularly scheduled game for that date. **(N)**

4.13 THE UMPIRE MAY DECLARE A GAME FORFEITED in favor of the opposing team when a team— **(24)**

(a) Fails to appear upon the field, or being upon the field, refuses to start play within five minutes after the umpire has called "Play" at the appointed hour for beginning the game, unless such delayed appearance is, in the umpire's judgment, unavoidable; **(24-1)**

(b) Employs tactics palpably designed to delay or shorten the game; **(24-4)**

(c) Refuses to continue play during a game unless the game has been suspended or terminated by the umpire; **(24-2)**

PENALTY

The manager responsible for his team's refusal to play shall be subject to a fine by the President of the League and suspension for a period of not less than 90 playing days. **(24-2)**

(d) Fails to resume play, after a suspension, within one minute after the umpire has called "Play;" **(24-3)**

(e) After warning by the umpire, wilfully and persistently violates any rules of the game; **(24-5)**

(f) Fails to obey within a reasonable time the umpire's order for removal of a player from the game; **(24-6, N)**

(g) Is unable or refuses to place nine players upon the playing field; **(24-7)**

(h) Fails to appear for the second game of a double-header within twenty minutes after the close of the first game unless the umpire-in-chief of the first game shall have extended the time of the intermission. **(24-9)**

4.14 A GAME SHALL BE FORFEITED TO THE VISITING TEAM if, after it has been suspended, the orders of the umpire to ground keepers respecting preparation of the field for resumption of play are not complied with. **(24-8)**

4.15 If the umpire declares a GAME FORFEITED he shall transmit a WRITTEN REPORT to the President of the League within twenty-four hours thereafter, but failure of such transmittal shall not affect the forfeiture. **(24-10)**

4.16 PROTESTING GAMES. Each league shall adopt rules governing procedure for protesting a game, when a manager claims that an umpire's decision is in violation of these rules. No protest shall ever be permitted on judgment decisions by the umpire.   **(56, 58)**

5.00—Putting the Ball in Play. Live Ball.

5.01 At the time set for beginning the game the umpire shall call "Play." **(66)**

5.02 The PITCHER shall deliver the PITCH TO THE BATTER who may elect to strike the ball, or who may not offer at it, as he chooses.   **(N)**

5.03 THE OFFENSIVE TEAM'S OBJECTIVE is to have its batter become a base runner, and its runners advance.   **(N)**

5.04 THE DEFENSIVE TEAM'S OBJECTIVE is to PREVENT OFFENSIVE PLAYERS FROM BECOMING BASE RUNNERS, or to prevent their advance around the bases.   **(N)**

5.05 When a BATTER BECOMES A RUNNER AND TOUCHES ALL BASES LEGALLY he shall SCORE ONE RUN for his team.   **(52)**

5.06 When THREE OFFENSIVE PLAYERS ARE LEGALLY PUT OUT, that team takes the field and the opposing team becomes the offensive team. **(N)**

5.07 After the umpire calls "Play" the BALL IS ALIVE and in play and remains alive and in play until for legal cause, or at the umpire's call of "Time" suspending play, the ball becomes DEAD. While the ball is dead no player may be put out, no bases may be run and no runs may be scored, except that runners may advance as legally provided.   **(N)**

5.08 If a thrown ball accidentally strikes a coacher, or a pitched or thrown ball strikes an umpire, THE BALL is ALIVE and in play.   **(47)**

5.09 THE BALL BECOMES DEAD and runners return, or advance, to their bases, without jeopardy or liability to be put out, when—

(a) A pitched ball touches a batter, or his clothing, while in his legal batting position; runners, if forced, advance;   **(32-1, 48-5)**

(b) The umpire back of home base interferes with the catcher's attempt to throw; runners return;   **(48-4)**

(c) A balk is committed; runners advance;   **(32-2)**

(d) A ball is illegally batted; runners return;   **(32-3, 48-2)**

(e) A foul is hit which is not caught; runners return;   **(32-4, 48-1)**

(f) Interference is called; runners return;   **(32-5)**

(g) A fair hit ball **touches a runner or an umpire** before it touches an infielder including the pitcher, or touches an umpire before it has passed an infielder other than the pitcher. If a fair ball goes through, or by, an infielder, and hits a runner immediately back of him, or hits a runner after being deflected by an infielder, the umpire must not declare the runner out for being hit by a batted ball. In making such decision the umpire must be convinced that the ball passed through, or by, the infielder and that no other infielder had the chance to make a play on the ball; runners advance, if necessary;   **(32-6, 48-6)**

(h) The coacher intentionally interferes with a thrown ball; runners return;   **(47-7, 48-8)**

(i) The ball touches spectator; runners advance;   **(32-7, 33)**

(j) Any legal pitch hits a runner trying to score; **runner advances.** **(47-9)**

5.10 THE BALL IS DEAD when the umpire-in-chief suspends play by CALL-ING "TIME" when—

(a) In his judgment RAIN, DARKNESS, OR OTHER CAUSE, makes further play immediately impossible. The umpire-in-chief shall have authority to call "Play" for resumption of the game whenever in his judgment, the condition of the playing field warrants it. After thirty minutes of such suspension the umpire shall have authority to termi-nate the game, but if, in his judgment, there is any chance to resume play he may continue such suspension as long as his judgment warrants. **(67-1)**

(b) An ACCIDENT INCAPACITATES A PLAYER OR UMPIRE, or if it is necessary to remove a player or spectator from the grounds. The umpire shall not call "Time" because of an accident to player or um-pire during a play until, in his judgment, no further action is possible in that play; **(67-2)**

(c) A MANAGER REQUESTS "TIME" for a substitution, or for con-ference with his player; **(N)**

(d) The umpire wishes to examine the ball, or FOR ANY SIMILAR CAUSE; **(32)**

(e) A fielder, after catching a fly ball, **FALLS** into a bench, dugout or stand, or falls across ropes into a crowd (when spectators are on the field), and base runners may advance one base without liability to be put out. (NOTE: If player after making the catch STEPS into the dugout but does not FALL, the ball is alive and in play and runners may advance at their own peril.) **(N)**

6.00—Rules Governing the Offense.

THE BATTER

6.01 Each player of the offensive team shall bat IN THE ORDER that his name appears in HIS TEAM'S BATTING ORDER. **(34)**

6.02 The BATTER'S LEGAL POSITION shall be with both feet within the batter's box. **(34)**

6.03 The FIRST BATTER IN EACH INNING after the first inning shall be the player whose name follows that of the last player who legally completed his time at bat in the preceding inning. **(36)**

6.04 A batter has legally completed his TIME AT BAT when he is put out or becomes a base runner. **(N)**

6.05 A BATTER IS OUT WHEN—

(a) His fair or foul fly ball (other than a foul tip) is legally caught by a fielder; **(44-3, 49-2-a)**

(b) A third strike is legally caught by the catcher; **(49-3)**

(c) He bunts foul on the third strike; **(44-9)**

(d) A third strike is not caught by the catcher; provided there is a runner on first base and not more than one is out; **(44-6)**

(e) He hits an Infield-Fly before two are out when runners occupy first and second bases, or first, second and third bases; **(44-8)**

(f) He attempts to hit a third strike and the ball touches him; **(44-7)**

(g) After striking or bunting the ball he INTENTIONALLY strikes the ball a second time, or strikes it with a thrown bat, or deflects its course

in any manner while running to first base. The ball is dead and no runners may advance. If the runner drops his bat and the ball rolls against the bat and, in the umpire's judgment, there was no intention to interfere with the course of the ball, the ball is alive and in play;
(49-2-b, N)

(h) After a third strike or a fair hit, he is tagged by any fielder before he touches first base, or the ball is held firmly in the hand or glove of any fielder on first base before the runner touches that base;   (49-4, 49-5)

(i) In running the last half of the distance from home base to first base while the ball is being fielded to first base, he runs outside (to the right of) the three-foot line, or inside (to the left of) the foul line, and in the umpire's judgment in so doing interferes with the fielder taking the throw at first base; except that he may run outside (to the right of) the three-foot line or inside (to the left of) the foul line to avoid a fielder attempting to field a batted ball;
(49-6)

(j) With less than two out and first, first and second or first, second and third bases occupied, a fielder intentionally drops a fly ball or line drive. The batter is out, runners need not re-touch and may advance at their own peril;
(49-2-a)

(k) A preceding runner shall, in the umpire's judgment, intentionally interfere with the play of a defensive player who is attempting to catch a thrown ball or to throw the ball in an attempt to complete any play;
(N)

(l) With two out, a runner on third base, and two strikes on the batter, the runner attempts to steal home base on a legal pitch and the ball strikes the runner in the strike zone. The umpire shall call "strike three," the batter is out and the run shall not count; with less than two out the umpire shall call "strike three," the ball is dead, and the run counts.
(N)

6.06   A BATTER IS OUT FOR ILLEGAL ACTION WHEN—

(a) He fails to take his position in the batter's box promptly. If he persists in unwarranted delay in taking his position the umpire shall direct the pitcher to deliver the ball to the bat and every such pitch shall be called "strike" by the umpire. If he enters the batter's box in the interval between any such pitches, the ball and strike count shall continue regularly, but if he has not entered the batter's box when three strikes are called he shall be declared "out";
(44-2, N)

(b) Either of his feet is outside the lines of the batter's box when he hits the ball;
(43)

(c) He steps from one batter's box to the other while the pitcher is in position ready to pitch;
(44-10)

(d) He attempts to hinder the catcher from fielding or throwing the ball by stepping outside the batter's box, or otherwise interferes with that player. He shall not be called out, however, if despite his interference, the catcher's throw results in a putout, or if the catcher's play results in a putout at home base;
(44-5)

(e) HE FAILS TO TAKE HIS POSITION AT THE BAT IN THE TURN IN WHICH HIS NAME APPEARS ON THE BATTING ORDER. But if the error is discovered the proper batter may replace the man at bat before the latter becomes a base runner, in which case the balls and strikes called must be counted in the "time at bat" of the proper batter.   (44-1)

Only the proper batter shall be declared out, and no runs shall be scored or bases run because of any act of the improper batter.

This rule shall not be enforced unless the error is discovered, the appeal be made by the Manager, or a player of the defensive team, and the out be declared before the ball be delivered to the batter next facing the pitcher.

Should the batter declared out under this section be the third out and his team be thereby put out, the proper batter in the next inning shall be the player who would have come to bat had the players been put out by ordinary play in the preceding inning.

BECAUSE OF THE CONFUSION CONNECTED WITH THE PROPER APPLICATION OF THIS RULE, THE FOLLOWING NOTES AND ILLUSTRATIONS ARE HEREBY GIVEN OFFICIAL STATUS

1. THE UMPIRE SHALL NOT direct the attention of any person to the presence in the batter's box of an improper batter. This rule is designed to require the constant vigilance of the opposition and the operation of the rule requires such vigilance upon the part of players and Managers of both teams.

2. FIVE BASIC MANDATES are clear in the rule:
   Assume a batting order as follows:
   1. Smith
   2. Jones
   3. Brown
   4. Williams
   5. Carlson

(A) A proper batter may replace a wrong batter at any time before he becomes a base runner;
   Who is the following batter? Approved Ruling:
   With two balls and two strikes on Jones, his team discovers that **Jones is the wrong batter** and that Smith is the proper batter. Jones' manager asks the umpire for "Time," sends Smith to the batter's box, Smith assumes the ball and strike count on Jones and play proceeds. Jones is the proper following batter after Smith.

(B) Such proper batter assumes the ball and strike count of the wrong batter;
   Who is the following batter? Approved Ruling:
   Jones, the wrong batter, hits a fair ball for three bases scoring all runners except himself. Brown comes to bat and a pitch is delivered to him. The defensive team now discovers that Jones batted out of turn but, since a pitch had been delivered to Brown, Jones' hit is legal and the runs count. If, however, **any player other than Brown** had come to bat after Jones and if before Smith, Williams or Carlson had become a base runner it had been discovered that that batter was the wrong batter, the proper batter could have replaced this wrong batter by assuming the ball and strike count. But, since Brown legally followed Jones in the batting order, he finishes his time at bat and is followed by Williams.

(C) If, after the wrong batter has completed his time at bat, and before a pitch is delivered to another batter, the defensive team makes its "appeal"—that is, calls attention of the umpire to the just completed time at bat of the wrong batter—the umpire shall nullify every advance, score, and any and all advantage gained by the offensive team as the result of the acts of the wrong batter;

Who is the following batter? Approved Ruling:

> Player Jones hits a triple, scoring all runners except himself. But, before the next pitch, the defensive team discovers that **Jones is the wrong batter.** The umpire shall declare Smith (the proper batter) out, shall declare that all runners who scored on Jones' triple must return to their bases and that no runs shall be scored on Jones' hit. **Jones is the proper following batter.**

(D) The "appeal" having been sustained by the umpire, he calls the PROPER BATTER out—that is, the batter who SHOULD have taken his place in the batter's box;

Who is the following batter? Approved Ruling:

> Player Jones strikes out, or flies out. If Jones was the wrong batter, and it is discovered **after** the first pitch to the following batter, then if Brown was the following batter the game proceeds, but if **any other player** followed Jones at bat, Brown would take improper batter's place, his ball and strike count, and the game would proceed. If Jones was discovered to be the wrong batter before Brown received the first pitch, then Smith, the proper batter, would be declared out, and Jones would be the following batter.

(E) That if the "appeal" is not made until after a pitch has been delivered to the batter that followed the wrong batter, no "appeal" can be made nor accepted by the umpire in which event all advances, runs or other advantages gained by the offensive team, as the result of the acts of its wrong batter, become legal.

Who is the following batter? Approved Ruling:

> Player Williams bats in place of Smith who is the proper batter. If the error is discovered before Williams becomes a base runner, Smith takes his proper place at bat assuming the ball and strike count created by Williams. But if the error is discovered after Williams becomes a base runner and before a pitch is delivered to the following batter, **then Smith is declared out** and Jones is the proper following batter. If Williams finished his time at bat and is on base, and if a pitch has been delivered to the batter who followed him then that batter, Carlson, is the proper following batter and the game proceeds.

The Rule is, therefore, simplified by remembering one basic fact: If the improper batter is discovered before he becomes a runner, or before the first pitch to the following batter, the situation may be rectified at once; but if the error is discovered **after** the improper batter is on base, and **after** the first pitch to the following batter, the game proceeds with each batter taking his place in turn as if there had been no improper batter anywhere in the batting order.

If, on the other hand, the improper batter is **legally discovered in time,** all advances made by the offensive team due to his action are nullified.

6.07 THE BATTER BECOMES A BASE RUNNER AND IS ENTITLED TO FIRST BASE WITHOUT JEOPARDY (NOT LIABLE TO BE PUT OUT) WHEN—

(a) "Four balls" have been called by the umpire;   (46-3, 47-1

(b) He is struck by a pitched ball which he is not attempting to hit unless he makes no attempt to avoid being hit by the ball. If he makes no attempt to avoid being hit by the ball, the umpire shall call the pitch "ball" or "strike" as the case may be; (46-4)

(c) The catcher interferes with him, unless he reaches first base on a fair hit, an error, or otherwise, and no other runner is forced by his reaching first base, in which case the play proceeds without reference to the interference; (46-5)

(d) A fair ball strikes the person or clothing of the umpire or a base runner on fair ground before touching a fielder, provided that if a fair ball strikes the umpire after having passed a fielder other than the pitcher or having been touched by a fielder (including the pitcher), the ball shall be considered in play. Also, if a fair ball strikes the umpire on foul ground, the ball shall be in play. (46-6, 47-1)

6.08 THE BATTER BECOMES A BASE RUNNER AND IS IN JEOPARDY (LIABLE TO BE PUT OUT) WHEN—

(a) He makes a fair hit; (46-1)

(b) "Three strikes" have been called by the umpire and the third strike is not caught, unless there is a runner on first base with not more than one out; (46-3)

(c) Although interfered with by the catcher he makes a base hit or reaches first base on an error, or otherwise, and no other runner is forced by his reaching first base; (46-5)

(d) A fair ball, after having passed a fielder other than the pitcher, or after having been touched by a fielder, shall strike an umpire or base runner on fair territory; (46-6, 47-1)

(e) A fair fly ball passes over a fence or into the stands at a distance from home base of 250 feet or more. Such hit entitles the batter to a home run when he shall have touched all bases legally. A fair fly ball that passes over a fence or into the stands at a point less than 250 feet from home base shall entitle the batter to advance to second base, only; (41-2)

(f) A fair ball, after touching the ground, bounds into the stands, or passes through or under a fence, or through or under a scoreboard, or through or under shrubbery, or vines on the fence, in which case the batter and the base runners shall be entitled to advance two bases; (41-3, N)

(g) Any fair ball which, either before or after striking the ground, passes through or under a fence, or through or under a scoreboard, or through any opening in the fence or scoreboard, or through or under shrubbery, or vines on the fence, in which case the batter and the base runners shall be entitled to two bases; (N)

(h) Any bounding fair ball is deflected by the fielder into the stands, or over or under a fence on fair or foul ground, in which case the batter and all base runners shall be entitled to advance two bases; (N)

(i) Any fair fly ball is deflected by the fielder into the stands, or over the fence into foul territory, in which case the batter shall be entitled to advance to second base; but if deflected into the stands or over the fence in fair territory, the batter shall be entitled to a home run; (N)

(j) He fails to return **at once** to first base after overrunning or oversliding that base. If he attempts to run to second he is out when tagged. If, after overrunning or oversliding first base he starts toward the dugout, or toward his position, and fails to return to his base **at once,** he is out, **on appeal,** when he or the base is tagged.   **(49-18)**

7.00—Rules Governing the Offense.

THE BASE RUNNER

7.01 A RUNNER ACQUIRES THE RIGHT TO AN UNOCCUPIED BASE when he touches it before he is out. He is then entitled to it until he is put out; or touches the next base; or is legally forced to vacate it for a succeeding runner.   **(45)**

7.02 In advancing, a runner shall TOUCH FIRST, SECOND, THIRD AND HOME BASE IN ORDER. If forced to return, he shall re-touch all bases in reverse order unless the ball is dead. In that case he may go directly to his original base. In running to first base he may overrun or overslide first base provided he return to the base at once.   **(45, 49-13)**

PENALTY

The runner is out if he fails to touch his legal base while advancing or reversing, when a defensive player shall touch him with the ball, or hold the ball in his hand or glove while touching the base illegally missed, or touching the original base. The umpire shall call such runner out ONLY ON APPEAL by a defensive player before the next pitch.

7.03 TWO RUNNERS MAY NOT OCCUPY A BASE, but if, while the ball is alive, two runners are touching a base, the second runner shall be out when tagged. The first runner is entitled to the base.   **(45-3**

7.04 EACH RUNNER, OTHER THAN THE BATTER, MAY WITHOUT LIABILITY OF BEING PUT OUT ADVANCE ONE BASE WHEN—

    (a) There is a balk;   **(47-3**

    (b) The batter's advance without liability of being put out forces the runner to vacate his base; or when the batter hits a fair ball that touches another runner or the umpire before such ball has been touched by or has passed a fielder, if the runner is forced to advance.   **(47-2,48-3**

    (c) He is obstructed by a fielder, including the catcher. The ball is in play with respect to all other runners;   **(47-4**

    (d) While he is attempting to steal a base, the batter is interfered with by the catcher.   **(47-8**

7.05 EACH RUNNER INCLUDING THE BATTER-RUNNER MAY WITHOUT LIABILITY OF BEING PUT OUT, ADVANCE—

    (a) To home base, scoring a run, if a fair ball goes over the field fence in flight and he touches all bases legally; or if a fair ball, which, in the umpire's judgment, would have cleared the field fence in flight is deflected by the act of a defensive player in throwing his glove, cap or any article of his apparel, the runner shall be awarded a home run.   **(41-1, N**

    (b) Three bases, if any batted ball is touched by a fielder's use of his cap, glove, or any part of his uniform while such article is detached from its proper place on his person. The ball is in play and the batter may advance to home base at his peril;   **(47-**

(c) Two bases, if a fair ball touches a spectator, or if it bounces or is deflected into the stands outside the first or third base foul lines; or if it goes through or under a field fence, or through or under a scoreboard, or through or under shrubbery, or vines on the fence; **(33)**

(d) Two bases, if a live thrown ball is touched by a fielder's use of his cap, glove, or any part of his uniform while such article is detached from its proper place on his person. The ball is in play; **(47-5)**

(e) Two bases, if a live thrown ball goes into the stands, or into a players' bench, or on a slanting part of the screen above the "break" on the backstop, or over, under, or through a field fence. The ball is dead; **(65-2)**

(f) Two bases when, with no spectators on the playing field, a thrown ball goes into a stand, or over or through a fence surrounding the playing field, or into the players' bench (whether the ball rebounds into the field or not), or remains in the meshes of a wire screen protecting the spectators. The ball is dead. When such thrown ball is the first throw by an infielder the umpire, in awarding such bases, shall be governed by the position of the runner, or runners, at the time the ball was pitched; but **if a play intervenes** between the first throw by an infielder and the throw into the stands, the umpire in awarding such bases, shall be governed by the position of the runner, or runners, at the time the throw was made into the stands. When the throw is made by an outfielder, or is the result of any following plays, or attempted plays, the award shall be governed by the position of the runner, or runners, when the last throw was made; (Note on "play intervenes"—Intervening play as used herein refers to a play, or an attempt to make a play, by an infielder on a runner before the throw is made.) **(65-2, N)**

(g) One base, if a ball, pitched to the batter, or thrown by the pitcher from his position on the pitcher's plate to a base to catch a runner, goes into a stand, or players' bench, or over or through a field fence or backstop, or is touched by a spectator. The ball is dead. **(N)**

7.06 (a) A batter who has become a runner is entitled to unimpeded progress as he advances around the bases. Whenever a defensive player impedes the runner in any way, unless he is attempting to field a batted ball or has the ball in his possession, the umpire shall call "OBSTRUCTION," the ball shall remain in play, and all runners shall be permitted to advance, without liability to be put out, to the bases which, in the judgment of the umpire, the runners would have reached had obstruction not been called. **(N)**

(b) In a "run-down" play if the runner's progress is impeded by any defensive player who does not have the ball in his possession, the umpire shall call "OBSTRUCTION" and the runner shall be entitled to occupy the base he is attempting to reach when the obstruction occurred. **(N)**

7.07 If, with a runner on third base and trying to score by means of a squeeze play or a steal, the catcher steps on, or in front of home base without possession of the ball, or touches the batter or his bat, the runner shall be awarded home base for interference, the pitcher shall be charged with a balk, the batter shall be awarded first base, and the ball is dead. **(47-9)**

7.08 ANY BASE RUNNER IS OUT WHEN—

(a) He runs more than three feet away from a direct line between bases to avoid being tagged, unless his action is to avoid interference with a fielder fielding a batted ball;   (49-7)

(b) He intentionally interferes with a thrown ball; or hinders a fielder attempting to make a play on a batted ball;   (49-8)

(c) He is tagged, when the ball is alive, while off his base. The ball must be securely held by the fielder before and after the tag. If the impact of the runner breaks the base loose from its legal position, "TIME" is automatically called;   (49-9)

(d) He fails to re-touch his base after a fair or foul ball is legally caught before he, or his base, is tagged by a defensive player. He shall not be called out for failure to re-touch his base after the first following pitch. This is AN APPEAL PLAY;   (49-10, 49-14)

(e) He fails to reach the next base before a defensive player tags him or the base, after he has been forced to advance by reason of the batter becoming a base runner. However, if a succeeding runner is put out on a force play, the force is removed and the runner must be tagged to be put out;   (49-11)

(f) He is hit by a batted ball before it has touched or passed an infielder. The ball is dead and no run may score, nor runners advance, except runners who are forced to advance by the batter becoming a base runner. No runner touching his base shall be out if hit by a ball that is declared an Infield-Fly, but the batter is out. If a runner is off his base when hit by a declared Infield-Fly ball, both he and the batter are out   (49-12)

(g) He attempts to score on a play in which the batter interferes with the play at home base with less than two out. With two out, the interference puts the batter out and no score counts;   (49-15)

(h) He passes a preceding runner before such runner is out;   (49-16)

(i) After he has acquired legal possession of a base, he or that base is tagged while he is running the bases in reverse order for the purpose of confusing the defense or making a travesty of the game. No runner may advance in this situation in the event of an error on this play by the defensive team;   (45-2, N

(j) In running or sliding for home base, he fails to touch home base and makes no attempt to return to the base, when a defensive player holds the ball in his hand, while touching home base, and appeals to the umpire for the decision.   (N

7.09 IT IS INTERFERENCE BY A BATTER OR BY A RUNNER WHEN—

(a) After a third strike he hinders the catcher in his attempt to field the ball;   (49-1

(b) After striking or bunting the ball he INTENTIONALLY strikes the ball a second time, or strikes it with a thrown bat, or deflects its course in any manner while running to first base. The ball is dead and no runners may advance. If the runner drops his bat and the ball rolls against the bat and, in the umpire's judgment, there was no intention to interfere with the course of the ball, the ball is alive and in play   (49-2-b, N

(c) Before two are out and a runner on third base, the batter hinders a fielder in making a play at home base; the runner is out; (49-15)

(d) Any member or members of an offensive team stand, or otherwise collect, around any base to which a runner is advancing, to confuse, interfere or add to the difficulty of the defensive player; (49-20)

(e) In the judgment of the umpire, the coacher at third base, or first base, by touching or holding the runner, physically assists him in returning to, or leaving, third base or first base. The runner, however, shall not be declared out if no play is being made on him; (49-17)

(f) With a runner on third base, the coacher leaves his box and acts in any manner to draw a throw by a defensive player; (49-19)

(g) In running the last half of the distance from home base to first base while the ball is being fielded to first base, he runs outside (to the right of) the three-foot line, or inside (to the left of) the foul line and in the umpire's judgment, interferes with the fielder taking the throw at first base, or attempting to field a batted ball; (49-6, N)

(h) He fails to avoid a fielder who is attempting to field a batted ball, or intentionally interferes with a thrown ball; provided, that if two or more fielders attempt to field a batted ball, and the runner comes in contact with one or more of them, the umpire shall determine which fielder is entitled to the benefit of this rule, and shall not declare the base runner out for coming in contact with a fielder other than the one the umpire determines to be entitled to field such a ball; (49-8, N)

(i) A fair hit ball touches him before touching a fielder. If a fair ball goes through, or by, an infielder, and hits a runner immediately back of him, or hits the runner after having been deflected by a fielder, the umpire must not declare the runner out for being hit by a batted ball. In making such decision the umpire must be convinced that the ball passed through, or by the infielder, and that no other infielder had the chance to make a play on the ball. If, in the judgment of the umpire, the runner deliberately and intentionally kicks such a hit ball on which the infielder has missed a play, then the runner must be called out for interference. (49-12, N)

PENALTY FOR INTERFERENCE

The runner is out and the ball is dead.

.10 ANY BASE RUNNER IS OUT, **ON APPEAL** BEFORE THE NEXT EGAL PITCH, WHEN—

(a) After a batted fly ball is caught, he fails to re-touch his base before he or his base is tagged; (49-10)

(b) With the ball in play, while advancing or returning to a base, he fails to touch each base in order before he, or a missed base, is tagged; (49-13)

(c) He overruns or overslides first base and fails to return to the base immediately, and he is tagged. (49-18)

.11 THE PLAYERS OR COACHERS OF AN OFFENSIVE TEAM SHALL 'ACATE any space needed by a defensive player who is attempting to field a atted or thrown ball.

PENALTY

Interference shall be called and the offensive player on whom the play is being made shall be declared out. (18-3)

7.12 Unless two are out, the STATUS OF A FOLLOWING RUNNER is no affected by a preceding runner's failure to touch a base. If, upon appeal, th preceding runner is the third out, no runners following him shall score. (45-4

8.00—Rules Governing the Defense.

PITCHING

8.01 LEGAL PITCHING DELIVERY. There are two legal pitching pos tions:

(a) The "Windup" Position, and

(b) The "Set Position"—and either position may be used at any time
(27-1, N

(a) The "Windup Position." The pitcher shall stand facing the batter, hi pivot foot on, or in front of and touching the pitcher's plate, and th other foot free. From this position any natural movement associate with his delivery of the ball to the batter commits him to the pitc without interruption or alteration. He shall not raise either foot fron the ground, except that in his actual delivery of the ball to the ba ter, he may take one step backward, and one step forward with hi free foot.

(b) The "Set Position." Set position shall be indicated by the pitcher whe he stands facing the batter with his entire pivot foot on, or in front o and in contact with, and not off the end of the pitcher's plate, and hi other foot in front of the pitcher's plate, holding the ball in botl hands in front of his body and **coming to a complete stop** of at leas one second. From such set position he may deliver the ball to the ba ter, throw to a base or step backward off the pitcher's plate with hi pivot foot. BEFORE assuming set position the pitcher may elect t make any natural preliminary motion such as that known as "th stretch." But if he so elects, he must come to set position before de livering the ball to the batter. AFTER assuming set position, any na ural motion associated with his delivery of the ball to the batter con mits him to the pitch without alteration or interruption.   (27-1, N

(c) At any time during the pitcher's preliminary movements and until hi natural pitching motion commits him to the pitch, he may throw t any base provided he **step directly toward such base before makin the throw.**
(31-2

(d) If the pitcher makes an illegal pitch with the bases unoccupied it sha be called a ball, unless the batter shall make a fair hit, or reaches fir base on an error or otherwise, and no other runner is forced by hi reaching first base.
(N

(e) If the pitcher removes his pivot foot from contact with the pitcher plate by stepping backward with that foot, he thereby becomes an ir fielder and, if his subsequent throw to a base, when off the pitcher plate, goes into a stand, or over, through or under a fence, or into bench or dugout (whether the ball rebounds or not), or remains i the meshes of a wire screen protecting the spectators, the ball is dea and all runners shall be entitled to advance two bases.
(N

8.02 THE PITCHER SHALL NOT BE ALLOWED TO—

(a) (1) Apply a foreign substance of any kind to the ball; (2) expectorat either on the ball or his glove; (3) rub the ball on his glove, person c clothing; (4) deface the ball in any manner; or to deliver what is called the "shine" ball, "spit" ball, "mud" ball or "emery" ball;   (27-2)

PENALTY

For violation of any part of this rule the umpire shall at once order the pitcher from the game, and in addition he shall be automatically suspended for a period of ten days, on notice from the President of the League.

(b) INTENTIONALLY DELAY THE GAME by throwing the ball to players other than the catcher, when the batter is in position, except in an attempt to retire a base runner;   (30-1)

PENALTY

If, after warning by the umpire, such delaying action is repeated, the pitcher shall be removed from the game.

(c) PITCH AT A BATTER'S HEAD, and if, in the umpire's opinion, such violation occurs, he shall call "Time" and warn the pitcher and the Manager of the defensive team that another such pitch will mean the immediate expulsion of the pitcher from the game. If such pitch is repeated the umpire shall inflict the—   (28, N)

PENALTY

The pitcher shall be removed from the game and from the grounds. The President of the League shall impose such fine and suspension as his judgment warrants.

(d) Pitch the "QUICK RETURN BALL." Whenever such pitch is attempted the umpire shall call "Time." If the offense is repeated the umpire shall call each such repeated offense a "ball," unless the batter reaches first base on a fair hit, an error, or otherwise, and no other runner is forced by his reaching first base, in which the play proceeds;   (N)

(e) Wear a garment with RAGGED, FRAYED OR SLIT SLEEVES, and shall not be permitted to attach tape or other material of a color different from his uniform, or glove, to his glove or clothing.   (N)

$.03 When a pitcher takes his position at the BEGINNING OF EACH INNING, or when he relieves another pitcher, he shall be permitted to pitch not o exceed eight preparatory pitches to his catcher during which play shall be uspended. Such preparatory pitches shall not consume more than one minute f time.   (30-2, N)

$.04 If with the bases unoccupied, the pitcher delays the game by failing to leliver the ball to the batter within 20 seconds after assuming pitching posiion, the umpire shall call "ball."   (30-2)

$.05 IF THERE IS A RUNNER, OR RUNNERS, IT IS A BALK WHEN—

(a) The pitcher, while touching his plate, makes any motion naturally associated with his pitch and fails to make such delivery;   (31-1)

(b) The pitcher, while touching his plate, feints a throw to first base and fails to complete the throw;   (31-2)

(c) The pitcher, in pitching position, fails to step directly toward a base before throwing to that base;   (31-2)

   (d) The pitcher while on the pitcher's plate throws, or feints a throw t
        an unoccupied base, except for the purpose of making a play;   (31-2

   (e) The pitcher delivers the ball to the batter while his pivot foot is bac
        of, or not in contact with the pitcher's plate;   (31-3

   (f) The pitcher delivers the ball to the batter while he is not facing th
        batter;   (31-4

   (g) The pitcher makes any motion naturally associated with his pitc
        while he is not touching the pitcher's plate;   (31-5

   (h) The pitcher unnecessarily delays the game;   (31-6

   (i) The pitcher, without having the ball, stands on or astride the pitcher
        plate or while off the plate, he feints a pitch;   (31-7

   (j) The pitcher, after coming to his set position, removes one hand fro
        the ball other than in an actual pitch, or in throwing to a base; (31-9

   (k) The pitcher, while touching his plate, accidentally or intentionall
        drops the ball;   (31-11

   (l) The pitcher pitches while the catcher is not in the catcher's box
        (31-12

   (m) The pitcher delivers the pitch from "set position" without comin
        to a stop of one full second.   (N

PENALTY

   The ball is dead, and each runner advances one base without liability to
   be put out.   (31-13)

8.06   A DEFENSIVE PLAYER, other than the pitcher and the catcher, MA
OCCUPY ANY POSITION on the playing field in fair territory.   (18-1

9.00—Rules Governing the Umpire, His Rights, Duties
and Responsibilities

9.01   THE UMPIRE IS THE ACCREDITED REPRESENTATIVE OF TH
LEAGUE, the President of the League and of Professional Baseball, and a
such is entitled to, and shall have the authority to require the full and complet
co-operation of all persons directly or indirectly responsible for the preparatio
for and the playing of a game.   (5:

9.02   THE UMPIRE'S AUTHORITY to act in legal manner on all matter
pertaining to a game SHALL NOT BE QUESTIONED.   (5:

9.03   DECISIONS INVOLVING AN UMPIRE'S JUDGMENT MAY NO
BE APPEALED by a manager or player.   (56, 5:

9.04   A MANAGER OR CAPTAIN, ONLY, shall have the RIGHT T
PROTEST AN UMPIRE'S DECISION and seek its reversal on the claim tha
such decision is in conflict with these rules. If, upon such appeal, and after co
sultation with an associate umpire, an umpire be convinced that his decisio
was in conflict with these rules he shall reverse such decision.   (5(

9.05   NO UMPIRE SHALL INTERFERE WITH, CRITICIZE, OR SEE
TO REVERSE ANOTHER UMPIRE'S DECISION, except as he shall hav
been called into consultation by the umpire whose decision is involved.   (5(

9.06   If but ONE UMPIRE is assigned to a game, his DUTIES AND JURI
DICTION shall extend to all points on the playing field and to all matters co
ered by this code, and he shall occupy any part of the playing field which, i
his opinion, will enable him to discharge his duties.   (5'

.07 Whenever more than one umpire is assigned to a game, one umpire shall ɔe designated "UMPIRE-IN-CHIEF" and the others "FIELD UMPIRES." **(53)**

.08 The DUTIES of the UMPIRE-IN-CHIEF shall be to—

(a) Take full charge of, and be responsible for, the proper conduct of the game;

(b) Take his position back of the catcher and call and count balls and strikes;

(c) Call and declare fair balls and fouls except those commonly called by field umpires;

(d) Make all decisions on the batter;

(e) Make all decisions except those commonly reserved for the field umpires;

(f) Decide when a game shall be forfeited.   **(54)**

.09 The DUTIES OF THE FIELD UMPIRE shall be to—

(a) Take such position on the playing field as, in his judgment, is best suited for the rendering of impending decisions on the bases;

(b) Make all decisions on the bases except those specifically reserved to the umpire-in-chief;

(c) Take concurrent jurisdiction with the umpire-in-chief in calling "Time," balks, defacement or discoloration of the ball by the pitcher, or use of illegal pitch;

(d) Aid the umpire-in-chief in every manner in enforcing these rules and, excepting the forfeiture of the game, shall have equal authority with the umpire-in-chief in removing from the game such players as may violate these rules.   **(55)**

.10 UMPIRES SHALL NOT BE CHANGED during a game unless such :hange becomes necessary because of illness or injury.   **(59)**

.11 THE UMPIRE SHALL REPORT TO THE PRESIDENT OF THE ̤EAGUE WITHIN TWELVE HOURS after termination of a game all violaions of the rules and other incidents, including the reasons for the removal of ι Manager or player from the game.   **(61)**

.12 When any person is debarred from further participation in a game for a ′LAGRANT OFFENSE such as the use of obscene or indecent language, or an ιssault upon a player, coach, Manager or umpire, the umpire shall, within ɔur hours thereafter, forward full particulars to the President of the League. **(63)**

.13 Immediately upon being informed by the umpire that a Manager, :oacher, trainer or player was removed from a game, the President of the ̤eague shall impose such penalty as his judgment justifies and shall notify the ɔerson involved, and the Manager of the Club of which such person is a memɔer. In the event of the imposition of a fine and the failure of the person so ιned to pay to the Secretary of the League the amount of said fine within five lays after such notice, such person shall be debarred from participating in any ;ame or from sitting on a players' bench during a game, until such fine be paid. **(62)**

THE RULES OF SCORING

SCORING RULES COMMITTEE

Roscoe McGowen, N. Y. Times, Chairman

Dan Daniel,
  N. Y. World-Telegram

Halsey Hall,
  Minneapolis Star & Tribune

Charles Young,
  Albany Knickerbocker News

Tom Swope,
  Cincinnati Post

INDEX

10.00—The Scorer

10.01 (a) THE SCORER is an actual official of the game he is scoring, is a accredited representative of the League, is entitled to the respect and dignity o his office and shall be accorded full protection by the President of the League

(b) THE SCORER shall report to the President of the League any indignity expressed by manager, player, club employee, or club official in the cours of, or as the result of, the discharge of his duties.

(c) To promote uniformity in keeping the records of championship game Scorers shall conform to the instructions of this scoring code.

10.02 In making a box score of a game, each player's name and the fielding position or positions he has played shall be listed in the order in which h batted, or would have batted if the game ends before he gets to bat, followed b a tabulated record of each player's batting and fielding.

10.03 (a) The first column shall show the number of times each player batted during the game, but no time at bat shall be charged against a player when h is awarded first base on four called balls, for being hit by a pitched ball, o because of being interfered with by the catcher, or for being obstructed by th catcher or any other player, while en route to first base. A sacrifice also exempt a player from being charged with a time at bat.

(b) The second column shall show the number of runs, if any, made b each player.

(c) The third column shall show the number of safe hits, if any, made b each player.

(d) The fourth column shall show the number of putouts, if any, made b each player.

(e) The fifth column shall show the number of fielding assists, if any, mad by each player.

(f) The sixth column shall show the number of fielding errors, if any made by each player.

(g) All players inserted into each team's line-up as substitute batters or sub stitute runners shall be so designated by special symbols plus notations at the bottom of their team's tabulated record. The symbols a, b, c, d, etc., are recommended. It also is recommended that the notations should describe what the extra batters did, such as—a-Singled for ——— in sixth inning; b-Flied out for ——— in third inning; c-Forced ——— for ——— in seventh inning; d-Grounded out for ——— in ninth inning.

(h) The score by innings of each team follows the box score tabulations and precedes the summary in which should be listed the following items in this order:

(1) Runs batted in

(2) Two-base hits.

(3) Three-base hits.

(4) Home runs, together with the names of the pitchers off whom hit.

(5) Stolen bases.

(6) Sacrifices.

(7) Double plays.

(8) Triple plays.

(9) Number of runners left on base by each team.

(10) Number of bases on balls issued by each pitcher.

(11) Number of batters struck out by each pitcher. These shall be listed as "strikeouts."

(12) Number of hits and runs (also earned runs) allowed by each pitcher (if one or both teams use more than one pitcher), together with the number of innings pitched by each pitcher. If a team uses only one pitcher, list the number of earned runs he allowed.

(13) The names of any hit batters together with the names of the pitchers who hit them, if a team uses more than one pitcher.

(14) The number of wild pitches made.

(15) The number of passed balls made by the catchers.

(16) The name of the winning pitcher, if the winning team uses more than one pitcher.

(17) The name of the losing pitcher, if the losing team uses more than one pitcher.

(18) The names of the umpires, listed in this order: (a) plate umpire; (b) first base umpire; (c) second base umpire; (d) third base umpire.

(19) The time of game with any delays for rain, fog, snow, light failure or violent wind storm deducted.

(20) All individual and team records of any forfeited or tied game which has reached or exceeded legal length when ended shall become a part of the official averages except that no pitcher shall be credited with a victory or charged with a defeat.

(21) A box score is in balance (or proved) when the total of a team's times at bat, bases on ball received, hit batters, sacrifices and batters awarded first base because of interference or obstruction equals the total of that team's runs, players left on base and the other team's putouts.

RUNS BATTED IN

(i) A run batted in is a run which reaches home base safely because of a safe hit, sacrifice hit, infield putout or outfield putout, or which is forced over home plate by reason of the batter being struck by a pitched ball, or being awarded a base on balls or being awarded first base because of interference by the catcher. If a batter hits a home run with the bases empty, score both a home run and a run batted in. If, with less than two out, an error is made on a play on which a runner from third base ordinarily would score and does score, credit the batter with a run batted in.

(j) The batter shall not be credited with a run batted in if a run scores when he hits into a force double play, or into a double play in which the first baseman fields a fair hit ground ball, touches first base ahead of the batter for an out, then throws to second or third base retiring a second runner who has to be tagged.

BASE HITS

10.04 A base hit shall be scored under these circumstances:

(a) When a batter reaches first base (or any succeeding base) safely on a legally batted ball which settles on fair ground or strikes a fence behind fair ground before being touched by a fielder, or which clears a fence behind fair territory;

(b) When a batter reaches first base after hitting a ball with such force, or so slowly, that the pitcher or fielder attempting to make a play with it has no opportunity to do so;

(c) When a batter reaches first base safely on a batted ball which strikes either first base, second or third base before being touched by a fielder and bounces away from the reach of the fielder;

(d) When a batter reaches first base safely on a legally batted ball which has not been touched by a fielder and which is in fair territory when it bounds into the outfield unless in the scorer's judgment it could have been handled with ordinary effort;

(e) When a legally batted ball which has not been touched by a fielder becomes "dead" by reason of touching the person or clothing of a runner or umpire, except that when a runner is called out for having been struck by an "infield fly" the batter shall not be credited with a hit;

(f) When, in the scorer's judgment, the batter could not have been retired at first base by perfect fielding, when the fielder fails in an attempt to retire a preceding base runner;

(g) Always give the batter the benefit of the doubt. A safe course to follow being to score a hit when exceptionally good fielding of a batted ball fails to result in a putout;

(h) In no case shall a base hit be scored when a runner is forced out by a batted ball, or would have been forced out except for a fielding error. Nor shall a hit be scored when an infield batted ball results in another runner, who is attempting to advance one base, being retired, whether forced out or not.

(i) Score the play as a "fielder's choice" when a fielder uses a batted ball to retire a preceding base runner, or would have retired one with ordinary effort except for a fielding error, charging the batter with a time at bat, but no hit.

DETERMINING VALUE OF BASE HITS

10.05 Whether a safe hit shall be scored as a one-base hit, two-base hit, or a three-base hit when no error or putout results shall be determined as follows:

(a) It is a one-base hit if the batter stops at first base; it is a two-base hit if the batter stops at second base; it is a three-base hit if the batter stops at third base, but note this **exception**: the batter must, if attempting to take two or three bases on a safe hit by sliding, hold the last base to which he advances. If he overslides and is tagged out before getting back to the base safely he shall be given credit for only as many bases as he safely attained. If he overslides second base and is tagged out he shall be given a one-base hit; if he overslides third base and is tagged out he shall be given a two-base hit. If he runs past second base after reaching that base on his feet, attempts to return and is tagged out, he shall be given credit for a two-base hit. If he runs past third base after reaching that base on his feet, attempts to return and is tagged out, he shall be given credit for a three-base hit.

(b) If a batter is awarded three bases on a batted or bunted ball because a fielder has touched the ball with his glove, cap or any other part of his uniform while such article is detached from its proper place on his person, the scorer's judgment shall dictate whether the batter shall be given credit for a one-base hit, a two-base hit, a three-base hit or a home run. If the scorer believes the fielder could have, by ordinary effort, kept the hit from being good for more than one, two, or three bases he shall score it as a one-base hit or as a two-base hit or as a three-base hit and charge the fielder with an error. If, however, the scorer believes the hit would have been a legitimate home run, despite illegal use of equipment, he shall so score it if the batter touches all bases in the proper order.

(c) In no instance shall the batter be credited with a two-base hit or a three-base hit if he fails to advance a preceding runner. Example: Runner on first, batter makes long hit and reaches second base but runner is thrown out at third base. Score a one-base hit and credit batter with reaching second on the play.

(d) When a batter ends a game with a safe hit, other than a home run, which drives in as many runs as are necessary to put his team in the lead, he shall be credited with only as many bases on his hit as are advanced by the runner who scores the winning run, and then only if the batter runs out his hit for as many bases as are advanced by the runner who scores the winning run, touching each base in the proper order.

(e) If a batter ends a game with a home run out of the playing field and touches all the bases in their proper order his run, and also the runs of all other runners who were on base when the home run was hit, shall count in the final score even though this gives the team last at bat a winning margin in excess of one run.

(f) Should a batter, after making a safe hit, be called out for having failed to touch a base, the last base he reached safely shall determine if his hit is scored as a one-base hit, a two-base hit or a three-base hit. If he is called out for missing second base the hit shall be scored as a one-base hit. If he is called out for missing third base, his hit shall be scored as a two-base hit. If he is tagged out after missing home base his hit shall be scored as a three-base hit. If he is called out for missing first base he shall be charged with a time at bat but no hit.

SACRIFICE HITS

10.06 Score a sacrifice if, with less than two out, the batter advances one or more runners with a bunt and is retired at first base, or would have been retired except for a fielding error. In case a runner is forced out at any base on a bunt it shall be scored as a time at bat but no sacrifice.

(a) "Squeeze play" is the term designating a play when a team, with a runner on third base, attempts to score that runner by means of a bunt. It also is a "squeeze play" if an attempt is made to score a runner from second base by means of a bunt.

FIELDING RECORDS

10.07 A putout shall be recorded each time a defensive player catches a fly ball, whether fair or foul, a line drive or a thrown ball which retires a batter or runner, or when a fielder tags a runner with the ball when the runner is off the base to which he legally is entitled.

(a) Automatic putouts shall be credited to the catcher as follows:

(b) When a batter is called out by the umpire for an illegally batted ball when a batter is called out by the umpire for bunting foul for his third strike, when a batter is called out by an umpire for being struck by his own batted ball; when a batter is called out by an umpire for interfering with the catcher, when a batter is called out by an umpire for failing to bat in his proper turn. (Note exception in 10.14 (a).)

(c) Other automatic putouts shall be credited as follows:

(d) When a batter is called out on an Infield-Fly which is not caught, the putout shall be credited to the fielder whom the scorer believes could have made the putout;

(e) When a runner is called out for being struck by a fair ball (including an Infield-Fly) the putout shall be credited to the fielder nearest the ball;

(f) When a runner is declared out by an umpire for running out of line to avoid being tagged by the ball in the hands of a fielder, the putout shall be credited to the fielder whom the runner avoided;

(g) When a runner is declared out by the umpire for having interfered with a fielder, credit the putout to the fielder with whom the runner interfered, unless the fielder was in the act of throwing the ball when interfered with, in which case the putout shall be credited to the fielder for whom the throw was intended, and the fielder whose throw was interfered with shall be credited with an assist.

ASSISTS

10.08 An assist shall be credited to each player who throws or deflects a batted or thrown ball in such a way that a putout results, or would have resulted except for a subsequent error by a teammate, but only one assist and no more shall be credited to each player who throws or deflects the ball in a rundown play which results in a putout, or would have resulted in a putout, except for a subsequent error.

(a) Credit an assist to each player who throws or deflects the ball during a play which results in a base runner being called out for interference, or for running out of line.

(b) Do not credit an assist to a pitcher when, in legally delivering the ball to a batter, he helps to retire a base runner attempting to steal home.

(c) Situations will arise in which a wild throw shall be scored as an assist and not as an error while on some plays a wild throw shall be scored both as an assist and as an error.
Examples:

(1) Runner A steals second base as Batter B strikes out. Catcher throws past second base and A attempts to reach third base but is thrown out by an outfielder. Score assists for the catcher and outfielder as part of a double play and exempt the catcher from an error.

(2) With Runner A on first base, Batter B hits a grounder to second baseman, whose throw to shortstop forces A at second base. Shortstop's relay to first base is wild. B attempts to reach second base on the overthrow, but the ball is recovered and thrown to second base, where B is tagged out before reaching that base. Score assists for the shortstop and the player who returned the wildly thrown ball as part of a double play and exempt the shortstop from an error.

(3) Runner A is on first base and B on second when Batter C grounds to shortstop. A is forced at second base, B moves to third base on the play and continues to score when the relay is wide of first base. C attempts to reach second base on the overthrow, but is retired before reaching that base. Score assists for the infielder making the wild relay to first and also for the player who recovered the wild throw and returned the ball to second base as part of a double play, but also score an error for the infielder whose wild throw permitted B to advance more than the normal one base.

(4) Runner A is on first base when Batter B hits into a force-out, shortstop unassisted. Shortstop, trying to double B, throws past first base. B continues past second base but is retired attempting to reach third base. Score assists for the shortstop and the player who recovered the overthrow and threw out B at third base as part of a double play, but also score an error for the shortstop for permitting B to reach second base.

DOUBLE PLAY—TRIPLE PLAY

0.09 A double play is any two successive putouts which take place between the time a ball leaves a pitcher's hand and is returned to him while he is standing in the pitcher's box.

(a) A triple play is any three successive putouts which take place between the time a ball leaves a pitcher's hand and is returned to him while he is standing in the pitcher's box.

ERRORS

0.10 An error shall be scored for each misplay (fumble, muff or wild throw) which prolongs the time at bat of a batter, or which prolongs the life of a runner, or which permits a runner to advance one or more bases when perfect play would have resulted in the batter or the runner being retired.

(a) Certain misplays by the catcher and pitcher known as "passed balls" and "wild pitches" are not errors but items for the summary and are defined elsewhere in these rules.

(b) Errors are not charged when a batter is awarded first base because of a base on balls, or for being struck by a pitched ball, or if a runner, or runners, advance because of a passed ball or because of the pitcher making a balk or a wild pitch except: If a batter swings at a wild pitch for his third strike and thereby is enabled to reach first base, it shall be scored as a strikeout and also as an error for the pitcher and not a wild pitch; when a catcher muffs a third strike, thereby permitting a batter to reach first base, it shall be scored as an error for the catcher, not a passed ball, and as a strikeout.

(c) No error shall be charged against the catcher or any other player for making a wild throw in attempting to prevent a stolen base or any other advance by a runner, unless the scorer is convinced such wild throw permitted the runner to advance one or more bases. If the wild throw permits a runner to advance an extra base, or bases, one error shall be charged to the player making the wild throw.

(d) When any player throws wildly in attempting to complete a double play, or a triple play, no error shall be scored unless the throw is so wild that at least one additional base be gained. However, if a fielder muffs a thrown ball which, if held, would have completed a double play or a triple play, score an error for the player who drops the ball.

(e) An error shall be scored against any player who, on receiving a thrown ball in ample time to retire a batter or any other base runner on a force play does not touch the base as required by the rules.

(f) When a runner advances because of the failure of a fielder to stop, or try to stop, an accurately thrown ball, the fielder failing to stop the ball shall be charged with an error and not the player making the throw, provided there was occasion for the throw. If such throw be made to second base the scorer shall determine whether it was the duty of the second baseman or the shortstop to stop the ball, and he shall charge the error to the negligent player.

(g) No error shall be scored if any fielder, after dropping a fly ball, a line drive or a thrown ball recovers the ball in time to force out a runner at another base.

(h) Accurately directed throws, especially from the outfield, which strike a base runner or an umpire, or which take an unnatural bounce and permit a base runner or base runners to advance, shall be scored as errors for the player making the throw even though it appears to be doing an injustice to the thrower. Every base advanced by a base runner must be accounted for.

STOLEN BASES

10.11 A stolen base shall be credited to a runner whenever he advances one base unaided by a base hit, a putout, a forceout, a fielder's choice, a passed ball, a wild pitch or a balk, subject to the following exceptions:

(a) If a double or triple steal is attempted and one runner is thrown out before reaching and holding the base he is attempting to steal, no other runner shall be credited with a stolen base;

(b) A runner who is touched out after oversliding a base shall not be regarded as having stolen that base.

(c) If it is the scorer's judgment that a palpable muff of a thrown ball prevents a runner who is attempting to steal from being retired, it shall be scored as an error for the player muffing the throw, an assist for the player throwing the ball, and not a stolen base.

(d) No stolen base shall be scored when a runner advances solely because of the defensive team's indifference to his advancement.

(e) If a runner advances while the defensive team, unsuccessfully, is attempting to retire another runner who, in attempting to steal, evades being put out in a rundown play and returns to the base he originally occupied, a stolen base shall be credited to the runner who so advances.

(f) If a runner has started for a succeeding base before the pitcher delivers the ball and the pitch results in a wild pitch or a passed ball, credit the runner with a stolen base with this exception: If another runner also advances because of the pitch becoming a wild pitch or passed ball, the wild pitch or passed ball also shall be scored.

(g) If a runner, attempting to steal, is well advanced toward the base he attempting to steal and a balk is called on the pitcher, credit the runner with

tolen base and do not score the balk unless another runner who is not attempt-
ng to steal is advanced by the balk.

WILD PITCHES—PASSED BALLS

10.12 A wild pitch shall be scored when a legally delivered ball is so high, or
o wide, or so low that the catcher does not stop and control the ball by ordinary effort and, as a result, a runner or runners, advance.

(a) Any legally pitched ball which strikes the ground before reaching home
plate and passes the catcher, permitting a runner, or runners, to advance shall
be scored as a wild pitch.

(b) A catcher shall be charged with a passed ball when a runner, or runners, advance because of the catcher's failure to hold or to control a legally
pitched ball which should have been held or controlled with ordinary effort.

BASES ON BALLS

10.13 A base on balls shall be scored whenever a batter is awarded first base by
the umpire because of four balls having been pitched outside the strike zone,
but when the fourth such ball strikes the batter it shall be scored as a "hit
batter."

STRIKEOUTS

10.14 A strikeout shall be scored whenever a pitcher delivers three legal
pitches at which the batter swings and misses, or which the umpire decrees are
trikes even though the batter may reach first base safely after the third strike
by reason of a wild pitch or the catcher's failure to hold the ball.

(a) A strikeout shall be scored whenever a batter bunts foul when there are
wo strikes against him, except that should the bunt result in a foul fly caught
by the catcher or any other player it shall not be scored as a strikeout but as a
regular foul-fly putout.

(b) When a batter goes out of the game with two strikes against him and
he substitute batter completes a strikeout, score it as a strikeout for the first
batter. If the substitute batter completes the turn at bat in any other manner,
core the action as having been that of the substitute batter.

EARNED RUNS

10.15 An earned run is a run for which the pitching is held accountable.

(a) An earned run shall be scored every time a player reaches home base
by the aid of safe hits, sacrifices, stolen bases, putouts, bases on balls, hit batters,
balks or wild pitches (even though a wild pitch be a third strike which enables
batter to reach first base), before fielding chances have been offered to retire
he offensive team.

(b) Since a wild pitch on which a batter reaches first base is the pitcher's
fault, solely, even though it is scored as a fielding error, it shall be disregarded
as an error and considered as a wild pitch in computing earned runs and is the
only instance in which an error is so disregarded.

(c) In computing earned runs any type of fielding error made by a pitcher
other than the one mentioned in the preceding two paragraphs) shall be con-
idered in the same light as an error by any other fielder.

(d) Whenever a fielding error occurs the pitching shall be given the bene-
t of the doubt in determining to which bases any base runners would have
dvanced had the fielding by the defensive team been errorless.

(e) No run can be earned which scores as a result of a batter having reached first base safely because of a catcher's interference, or because of an fielding error, except a wild pitch as noted in Section (b) above.

(f) When pitchers are changed during an inning the preceding pitcher and not the relieving pitcher, shall be charged with any earned or unearned runs scored by any runners on base when such relief pitcher entered the game There is, however, this exception: If the action of any batter to whom th relieving pitcher pitches results in the retirement of a runner left on base b the preceding pitcher, the batter whose action resulted in the retirement of tha runner shall be considered as having been left on base by the preceding pitche and any run scored by such runner shall be charged to the preceding pitcher

(g) A relieving pitcher shall not be held accountable for the first batter to whom he pitches reaching first base if that batter had a decided advantag because of ineffective pitching by the pitcher whom the relieving pitcher suc ceeded. Thus, if the count is two or three balls and one or no strikes, or if th count is three balls and two strikes when pitchers are changed, and the batte reaches first base safely, charge that batter to the pitcher who was replaced. I such a batter is retired, or would have been retired except for a fielding error the batter shall be credited to the relieving pitcher. Likewise, if such a batte hits into a forceout or into a fielder's choice on which a runner is retired, o would have been retired except for a fielding error, credit the action of such batter to the relieving pitcher. (The foregoing sentence is not to be construe as affecting or conflicting with the exception noted in preceding section (f). If pitchers are changed when the count is two balls and one or no strikes, o one ball and one or no strikes, the relieving pitcher shall be held accountabl for whatever the batter does.

DETERMINING WINNING AND LOSING PITCHER

10.16 Determining the winning and losing pitcher of a game often calls fo much careful consideration.

(a) Do not give the starting pitcher credit for a game won, even if th score is in his favor, unless he has pitched at least five innings when replaced

(b) The five-inning rule to determine a winning pitcher shall be in effe for all games of six or more innings. When a game is called after five innings o play the starting pitcher must have pitched at least four innings to be credite with the victory.

(c) If the starting pitcher is replaced (except in a five-inning game) befor he has pitched five complete innings when his team is ahead, remains ahead t win, and more than one relief pitcher is used by his team, the scorer shall cred the victory (as among all relieving pitchers) to the pitcher whom the score considers to have done the most effective pitching. If, in a five-inning game, th starting pitcher is replaced before pitching four complete innings when h team is ahead, remains ahead to win, and more than one relief pitcher is use by his team, the scorer shall credit the victory (as among all relieving pitcher to the pitcher whom the scorer considers to have done the most effectiv pitching.

(d) Regardless of how many innings the first pitcher has pitched, he sha be charged with the loss of the game if he is replaced when his team is behin in the score, and his team thereafter fails to either tie the score or gain the lea

(e) If a pitcher retires from the game for a substitute batter, or a substitut runner, after pitching five or more innings and his team scores enough runs in the inning in which he is replaced to take the lead, those runs shall be credited to his benefit. Thus, if a pitcher is removed for a substitute batter or a substitute base runner in any inning after the pitcher has pitched at least five complete innings and during the inning in which he is removed his team assumes the lead, he shall be credited with the victory if his team remains ahead until the finish of the game.

(f) Examples: If the pitcher of the team first at bat is removed in the first half of the sixth inning for a substitute batter, or a substitute runner, and his team gains the lead in that inning and the relieving pitcher holds the lead through the last half of the ninth inning, the pitcher who was removed shall be credited with the victory; if the pitcher of the team last at bat is removed in the last half of the fifth inning for a substitute batter, or a substitute runner, and his team gains the lead in that inning with the relieving pitcher holding the lead through the ninth inning, the pitcher who was removed shall be credited with the victory.

(g) In giving a pitcher credit for the number of innings pitched divide each inning into three parts. Thus, if a pitcher is replaced, with one opponent out, in the sixth inning the pitcher so replaced shall be credited with having pitched 5 1-3 innings. If a pitcher is replaced with none out in the opposing team's sixth inning he shall be credited with having pitched 5 innings and a notation made to the effect that there were none out in the sixth inning.

DETERMINING PERCENTAGES

10.17 To determine a pitcher's earned run prevention average for a season the total number of earned runs charged against his pitching shall be divided by the total number of innings he has pitched then multiplied by nine to find his average effectiveness for a complete game.

(a) To determine the percentage of games won and lost divide the total number of games won and lost into the number won.

(b) To determine a batting average, divide the total "times at bat" into the total number of safe hits.

(c) To determine a slugging percentage, divide the total "times at bat" into the total bases of all safe hits.

(d) To determine a fielding average, divide the total of putouts, assists and errors into the total of putouts and assists.

BATTING CHAMPIONSHIPS

10.18 To be eligible for the individual batting championship of any minor league, a player must have appeared in at least two-thirds of the games played by his team. Thus, if a team plays 154 games, a player must appear in 102 games. If his team plays 150 games he must appear in 100. If his team plays 140 games he must appear in 93, etc.

(a) To be eligible for the individual batting championship of a major league a player must be credited with at least 400 official "times at bat."

NOTES — CASEBOOK — COMMENT

The following is intended as a helpful explanation of points in the Rules wherever the Rules, themselves, do not provide clear and indisputable answers. These notes are given the same Official Status by the Committee as is given to the Rules.

The Rules Committee acknowledges with gratitude the labors of the Sub-Committee on Recodification consisting of Warren C. Giles, Frank J. Shaughnessy, Joseph E. Cronin, Thomas H. Connolly and Robert L. Finch. This Committee gave careful consideration to the many suggestive changes and prepared the text for final approval by the Official Rules Committee.

The Rules Committee is also indebted to many others in the Professional, Semi-Professional and Amateur field whose study of the first draft resulted in many corrections and clarifications.

THE OFFICIAL BASEBALL RULES COMMITTEE
George M. Trautman, Chairman

1.01 ENCLOSED FIELD. Required by professional leagues only, but preferable everywhere.
1.07 THE DIAGRAM. Heavy lines indicate which **must** be marked before the game begins. There is no substitute for grass in the infield.
1.10 BASES. A pleasing innovation has been the placing of clean, white bases in position after the preliminary practice is concluded and just before each game begins. This "dresses up" the park and makes umpiring more accurate.
1.14 THE BAT must not be loaded with metal fillings. It is illegal.
1.15 UNIFORMS. The baseball uniform is a distinctive institution. Players and patrons have every reason to honor the uniform. Players should wear the uniform properly. Managers should insist that baseball pants be anchored just below the knee and that the slovenly custom of anchoring the pant leg around the ankle shall cease. Tattered, dirty uniforms disgrace the game. It is recommended that when players wear undershirts or jerseys, they should be uniform in color.
2.05 If the pitch strikes the ground and bounces through the strike zone it is a "ball." If such a pitch hits the batter he is entitled to first base. If the batter elects to strike at such bounding pitch, the ensuing action shall be same as if the ball were in flight.
2.23 If a fly ball lands in the infield between home and first base, or home and third base, and then bounces to foul territory without touching a player or umpire and before passing first or third base, it is a foul ball; or if the ball settles on foul territory or is touched by a player on foul territory, it is a foul ball. If any defensive player fields such a foul ball in foul territory and throws the ball to first base, the batter is not out. If a fly ball lands on or beyond first or third base and then bounces to foul territory, it is a fair hit.
Clubs, increasingly, are erecting tall foul poles at the fence line with a wire netting extending along the side of the pole on fair territory above the fence to enable the umpires more accurately to judge fair and foul balls. The custom should become universal.
2.27 FORCE PLAY. Confusion regarding this play is removed by remembering that frequently the "force" situation is **removed during the play.** Example: Man on first, one out, ball hit sharply to first baseman who touches the bag and batter-runner is out. The force is removed at that moment and runner advancing to second must be tagged. If there had been a runner on third or second, and either of these runners scored before the tag-out at second, the run counts. Had the first baseman thrown to second and the ball then had been returned to first, the play at second was a force out, making two outs, and the return throw to first ahead of the runner would have made three outs. In that case, no run would score.
Example: **NOT A FORCE OUT.** One out and runners on first and third. Batter flies out. Two out. Runner on third tags up and scores. Runner on first tries to retouch before throw from fielder reaches first baseman, but does not get back in time and is out. Three outs. If, in umpire's judgment, the runner from third touched home base before the ball was held at first base, the run counts.
2.29 Approved Ruling: The exact **position of the ball** determines whether it is foul or fair, not the position of the fielder's body when he touches the ball.

Approved Ruling: Without touching a fielder, a batted ball hits pitcher's rubber and rebounds over catcher's head, or to foul territory between home and first, or between home and third base. This is a foul.

2.36 If at a given moment **the center fielder,** for instance, is playing in a position ordinarily occupied by an infielder, or in any position adjacent to the bases, he **is** in that moment **an infielder.**

2.37 The Infield-Fly rule is a device to prevent one, single unfair situation, i.e., a double play when the offensive has no possible method of escape. Umpires must be accorded time for the decision if a wind is blowing; they must be expected to reverse the call, if the ball drops foul. Under normal conditions, however, the declaration should be made at the earliest reasonable moment so that runners may act. Major league umpires call "Infield-Fly, if Fair!" on balls close to the baseline.

2.40 A team's time at bat is **one-half of an inning.** The other half inning is the duration of the time at bat of the opposing team.

2.51 **Distinguish** clearly the **difference** between a **pitch and a thrown ball.** A pitch is exclusively the delivery of the ball to the batter. All other deliveries of the ball by one player to another are thrown balls.

2.63 **The Strike Zone.** A batter has the right to expect that the area he is protecting shall be the same from day to day. Necessity for split-second decision by the batter makes it imperative that umpires practice diligently to attain a sameness in their estimation of the strike zone. A crouch, assumed to confuse the pitcher, or to lower and narrow the natural-stance space for the reception of the pitch, shall be disregarded by the umpire. However, a batter's natural batting stance may be an exaggerated crouch.

3.01 (b) **The Catcher's Box must be included in the lines to be marked.**

3.01 (e) (3) After dead ball and when all play has ceased, the umpire shall deliver the alternate ball to the pitcher. Play shall not be resumed with an alternate ball when a fair batted ball or a ball thrown by a fielder goes out of the ground or into a stand for spectators until the runners have completed the circuit of the bases unless compelled to stop at second or third base in compliance with a ground rule. Alternate balls shall be reintroduced into the game in the order of their return to the umpire. He shall call for a new ball only when the supply of alternate balls is exhausted.

3.02 An additional reason why **umpires must keep the ball constantly in view.**

3.08 Players for whom **substitutions** have been made may remain with their team on the bench or may "warm-up" pitchers. If a Manager substitutes another player for himself, he may continue to direct his team from the bench or the coacher's box. Major league umpires do not permit players for whom substitutions have been made, and who are permitted to remain on the bench, to address any remarks to any opposing player or manager, or to the umpires.

3.11 The basic reason for baseball's hold upon its patrons is the **competitive nature of the game;** the traditional assurance that when a baseball game is played, the teams forget all else except to win in a sportsmanlike manner. Any mingling with spectators or fraternization by opposing players tends to destroy this conviction.

3.17 The nature of a baseball game requires discipline. Confusion, "incidents" and a variety of unhappy experiences are bound to occur if players are not **restricted to the bench.** Umpires should enforce this rule.

3.18 "Reasonable length of time" as used in this code always means that the umpire-in-chief shall be the sole judge of what **is** a reasonable length of time after the expiration of 15 minutes.

Forfeitures should always be the last resort of the umpire-in-chief after consultation with his colleagues. Every other resource should be exhausted before forfeiture. Patrons pay to see a game. They should not be disappointed.

4.01 (d) **Batting Orders** are exchanged and each manager must be accorded an opportunity to examine his opponent's lineup. At the moment the umpire receives the home manager's batting order, the umpire assumes complete control of the playing field. Thereafter there shall be no change in batting orders except by the substitution method.

4.07 When **Manager, player or other team member is removed from the game,** he shall not sit in the stands adjacent to his team's bench.

4.09 Baseball is so genuinely **a team game** that an error of omission, as well as an error of commission, can, and frequently does, nullify the brilliant individual play of a teammate. This emphasizes the team-play character of the game.

Approved Ruling: No run shall be scored on a play in which the third out is made on the batter before he reaches first base, safely. Example: One out, Jones on second, Smith on first and the batter, Brown, hits safely. Jones easily crosses the plate. Smith, on the throw to the plate, is out. Two outs. But Brown missed first base (and, therefore, did not "reach first base safely"). The ball is thrown to first, an appeal is made and Brown is out. Three outs. But, since Jones crossed the plate "on a play in which the third out was made on the batter before he reached first base safely," **Jones' score does not count.**

Approved Ruling: Succeeding runners are not affected by an act of a preceding runner unless two are out.

Example: One out, Jones on second, Smith on first, and batter, Brown, hits home run inside the park. Jones fails to touch third on his way to the plate. Smith and Brown score. The defense holds the ball on third, appeals to umpire, and Jones is out. Smith's and Brown's runs count.

Approved Ruling: Two out, Jones on second, Smith on first and batter, Brown, hits home run inside the park. All three runs cross the plate. But Jones missed third base, and on appeal is declared out. Three outs. Smith's and Brown's runs are voided. No score on the play.

Approved Ruling: One out, Jones on third, Smith on second. Batter Brown flies out to centerfield. Two outs. Jones scores after catch and Smith scores on bad throw to plate. But Jones, on appeal, is adjudged to have left third before the catch and is out. Three outs. No runs.

Approved Ruling: Two out, bases full, and batter hits home run over the fence. Batter on appeal, is declared out for missing first base. Three outs. No run counts.

Here is a general statement that covers:

When a runner misses a base and a defensive player holds the ball on a missed base, or on the base originally occupied by the runner, and appeals for the umpire's decision, the runner is out when the umpire sustains the appeal; all runners may score if possible, except that with two out the runner is out at the moment he misses the bag, if an appeal is made, as applied to succeeding runners.

Approved Ruling: One out, Jones on third, Smith on first, and Brown flies out to right field. Two outs. Jones tags up and after the catch, scores. Smith attempted to return to first but the rightfielder's throw beat him to the base. Three outs. **But,** Jones had scored **before** the throw to catch Smith reached first base, hence Jones' run counts. It was **not** a force play.

4.13 (b) Tactics by Managers or players of either or both teams **palpably designed to delay or shorten** a game in order to profit by such delay or shortening, are contrary to the great tradition of the game. The game shall be fought to its conclusion—"until the last man is put out." Any farcical lessening of effort by anybody on the playing field is high treason to the **s**pirit of good sportsmanship as exemplified by baseball.

4.13 (c) The **Manager is responsible** for the actions of his players on the field.

4.16 Managers contemplating protests should remember that a game may be protested **only** on the ground of violation of the rules. **Judgment decisions by the umpire offer no ground for a protest.**

5.09 (g) If a batted ball hits an umpire working in the infield after it has bounded past, or over, the pitcher, it is a dead ball.

5.10 (a) The umpire-in-chief shall, at all times try to complete a game. His authority to resume play following one or more suspensions of as much as thirty minutes each shall be absolute and he shall terminate a game only when there appears to be no possibility of completing it.

6.02 The batter **leaves the batter's box** at the risk of having a strike delivered and called, unless he requests the umpire to call "Time." The batter is not at liberty to step in and out of the batter's box at will.

6.05 (a) Read 2.14. The catch is legal if the ball is finally held by a fielder, even though juggled, or held by another fielder, **before it touches the ground.** Runners may leave their bases the instant the first fielder touches the ball. A fielder may reach over a fence, railing, rope or other line of demarcation to make a catch. He may jump on top of a railing, or canvas that may be on foul ground. No interference should be allowed where a fielder or catcher reaches over a fence, railing, rope or into a stand to catch a ball. He does so at his own risk. However, should a spectator reach out on the playing field side of such fence, railing or rope and plainly prevent fielder from catching the ball, then the batter should be called out for spectator's interference. If the fielder, or any defensive player should **fall** into the stand, or **fall down** in the dugout after making the catch, the ball is dead, and runners may advance one base without liability of being put out. If a player, after making the catch, **steps into the** dugout, **but does not fall,** the ball is alive and in play and runners may advance at their own peril.

6.05 (b) **"Legally caught" means in the catcher's glove.** It is not legal if the ball lodges in his clothing or paraphernalia; or if it strikes the umpire and is caught by the catcher on the rebound. If, on the third strike (not a foul tip) the ball passes the catcher and lodges in the umpire's mask or other paraphernalia the ball is dead, but the batter shall be entitled to first base and other runners shall advance one base.

6.05 (k) The objective of this rule is to penalize the offensive team for deliberate, unwarranted, unsportsmanlike action by the runner in leaving the baseline for the **obvious purpose** of crashing the pivot man on a double play, rather than trying to reach his base. Obviously this is an umpire's judgment play.

6.07 **The batter becomes a runner instantly** after he is required or entitled to reach first base. He is a runner instantly after he does something or something is done to him, that entitles him to reach first base. This code frequently refers to this person as the "batter" when a better term would be "batter-runner."

6.08 (j) Oversliding or overrunning situations arise at bases other than first base. For instance, with one or none out and runners on first and second, or first, second and third, the ball is hit to an infielder who tries for the double play. The runner on first beats the throw to second base but overslides the base. The relay is made to first base and the batter-runner is out. The first baseman, seeing the runner at second base off the bag, makes the return throw to second and the runner is tagged off the base. Meanwhile runners have crossed the plate. The question is: Is this a force play? Was the force removed when the batter-runner was out at first base? Do the runs that crossed the plate during this play and before the third out was made when the runner was tagged at second, count? Answer: The runs score. It is not a force play. It is a tag play.

7.04 (c) **The catcher, without the ball in his possession,** has no right to block the pathway of the runner attempting to score. The base line belongs to the runner and the catcher should be there only when he is fielding a thrown ball or when he already has the ball in his hand.

7.05 (b) The thrown glove or cap, etc., must **touch** the batted ball. There is no penalty if the thrown article does not touch the ball.

7.06 (a) Running is as much a part of baseball as hitting, fielding and throwing. All runners must be protected in their right to go as far as the action of the play, their speed and their daring dictates. It is not only unsportsmanlike to deny them this right, but it is highly dangerous to the runners to be subjected to intentional obstruction.

7.08 (b) A runner who is adjudged to have hindered a fielder who is attempting to make a play on a batted ball is out **whether it was intentional or not.**

7.08 (d) Runners need not "tag up" on a foul tip. They may steal on a foul tip. If a so called foul tip is not caught, it becomes an ordinary foul. Runners then return to their bases.

7.08 (f) If two runners are hit by the same fair ball, only the **first one is out** because the ball is instantly dead.

7.10 Umpires shall not recognize a "fourth out." If the third out is made on a play in which there is an immediate appeal play on another runner, and the appeal is sustained by the umpire, the appeal play decision takes precedence over the other play. If the third out on appeal is a force-out, or a failure of a runner to reach first base, no runs can score on the play. If the third out on appeal is not a forceout or failure of a runner to reach first base, the runs made before the appeal shall count.

APPROVED RULING: Jones on first base, Brown on second base, Smith on third base, two out. The batter, Williams, hits clean single to the outfield. Jones, advancing from first base, misses second base but on the throw-in is tagged sliding into third base. Two runs have crossed the plate, Brown and Smith, BUT, the second baseman calls for the ball, holds it on second base and appeals to the umpire, who sustains the appeal, calling Jones out for missing second base on a force out. Jones is the third out and no runs score.

8.01 (b) The pitcher in "set position" must face the batter with the foot other than his pivot foot in front of a line which is an extension of the front edge of the pitcher's plate.

8.01 (c) The pitcher must step **"ahead of the throw."** A snap throw followed by the step directly toward the base is a balk.

8.01 (c) But if the pitcher, **while off the rubber,** throws to any base he may do so at will and in case his throw goes wild and goes into a stand, etc., such throw is the throw of a fielder and what follows is governed by the rules covering a ball thrown by a fielder.

8.02 (a) All umpires must carry with them one Official Rosin Bag. The umpire-in-chief is responsible for placing the rosin bag on the ground back of the pitcher's plate. If at any time the ball hits the rosin bag it is in play. In the case of rain or wet field, the umpire may instruct the pitcher to carry the rosin bag in his hip pocket. A pitcher may use the rosin bag for the purpose of applying rosin to his bare hand or hands. Neither the pitcher nor any other player shall dust the ball with the rosin bag; neither shall the pitcher, nor any other player, be permitted to apply rosin from the bag to his glove, or dust any part of his uniform with the rosin bag.

8.02 (b) Pitchers, particularly non-professionals, most frequently **delay the game** by taking their catcher's signs from positions off the pitcher's rubber. This is a bad habit and should be corrected by managers and coaches.

8.02 (c) To pitch at a batter's head is unsportsmanlike and highly dangerous. It should be —and is—condemned by everybody. Umpires should act without hesitation in enforcement of this rule.

GENERAL INSTRUCTIONS TO UMPIRES

9.00 Umpires, on the field, should not indulge in conversation with players. Keep out of the coaching box and do not talk to the coach on duty.

Keep your uniform in good condition. Be active and alert on the field.

Be courteous, always, to club officials; avoid visiting in club offices and thoughtless familiarity with attaches of contesting clubs. When you enter a ball park your sole duty is to umpire a ball game as the representative of baseball.

Do not allow criticism to keep you from studying out bad situations that may lead to protested games. Carry your Rule Book. It is better to consult the Rules and hold up the game ten minutes to decide a knotty problem than to have a game thrown out on protest and re-played.

Keep the game moving. A ball game is often helped by energetic and earnest work of the umpires.

You are the only official representative of baseball on the ball field. It is often a trying position which requires the exercise of much patience and good judgment, but do not forget that the first essential in working out of a bad situation is to keep your own temper and self-control.

You no doubt are going to make mistakes, but never attempt to "even up" after having made one. Make all decisions as you see them and forget which is the home or visiting club.

Keep your eye everlastingly on the ball while it is in play. It is more vital to know just where a fly ball fell, or a thrown ball finished up, than whether or not a runner missed a base. Do not call the plays too quickly, or turn away too fast when a fielder is throwing to complete a double play. Watch out for dropped balls after you have called a man out.

Do not come running with your arm up or down, denoting "out" or "safe." Wait until the play is completed before making any arm motion.

Each umpire team should work out a simple set of signals, so the proper umpire can always right a manifestly wrong decision when convinced he has made an error. If sure you got the play correctly, do not be stampeded by players' appeals to "ask the other man." If not sure, ask one of your associates. Do not carry this to extremes, be alert and get your own plays. But remember! The first requisite is to get decisions correctly. If in doubt don't hesitate to consult your associate. Umpire dignity is important but never as important as "being right."

A most important rule for umpires is always "BE IN POSITION TO SEE EVERY PLAY." Even though your decision may be 100% right, players still question it if they feel you were not in a spot to see the play clearly and definitely.

Finally, be courteous, impartial and firm, and so compel respect from all.

9.03 There shall be no appeal from the decision of the umpire-in-chief on a half swing. His decision must and will be final, it being entirely a question of the umpire's judgment as to whether the batsman struck at the pitch.

INDEX TO PLAYING RULES

— E —

— F —

— G —

— J —

— L —

— M —